TOWARD AN AMERICAN
CATHOLIC MORAL THEOLOGY

Other Books by Charles E. Curran

Directions in Fundamental Moral Theology
Directions in Catholic Social Ethics
Critical Concerns in Moral Theology
American Catholic Social Ethics: Twentieth-Century
  Approaches
Moral Theology: A Continuing Journey
Transition and Tradition in Moral Theology
Issues in Sexual and Medical Ethics
Catholic Moral Theology in Dialogue
New Perspectives in Moral Theology

Toward an American Catholic Moral Theology

CHARLES E. CURRAN

UNIVERSITY OF NOTRE DAME PRESS
NOTRE DAME, IN

Library of Congress Cataloging in Publication Data

Curran, Charles E.
  Toward an American Catholic moral theology.

  A collection of previously published essays.
  Includes index.
  Contents: Moral theology looks at itself: The historical
development of moral theology. Moral theology in the
United States. [etc.]
  1. Christian ethics — Catholic authors. I. Title.
BJ1249.C842   1987   241'.042   86-40583
ISBN 0-268-01862-6

Manufactured in the United States of America

In gratitude to
students, colleagues, and friends
who have supported me
in my living, working, and worshipping
during twenty-one years
at The Catholic University of America

Contents

Preface

This book brings together nine essays that have been written during the last few years on important topics in moral theology. This book by its very nature does not pretend to give a systematic and unified treatment of moral theology. However, the essays in this volume focus on two very significant areas of interest in contemporary moral theology — the discipline of moral theology itself and ethical evaluations of important issues of our society.

The attempt to work toward an American Catholic moral theology is the one common thread that unites all these studies. Many of the following essays treat explicitly of factors influencing the development of moral theology in the United States or else deal with social issues confronting church and society in the United States. However, two words of caution are necessary. First, an American Catholic moral theology must see itself as intimately related to the entire Catholic understanding in its historical development and in its many different contemporary manifestations. The studies gathered together in this volume emphasize that an American Catholic moral theology must strive to recognize both the Catholic and the American aspects of the enterprise. Second, there is a problem with the very word American. Unfortunately there is no adjective in English corresponding to the noun United States. American embraces all of North and South America. However, because of the limits of language American is used here to designate the United States.

"Part One: Moral Theology Looks at Itself" develops my understanding of where contemporary moral theology is and what it is trying to do. Historical consciousness is often men-

ix

tioned in the following pages as one of the most important characteristics of contemporary moral theology. To understand contemporary moral theology one must know its historical development and its contemporary contexts. The first two chapters indicate how moral theology has developed since the existence of the manuals of moral theology beginning in the seventeenth century and how the ecclesial, societal, and academic contexts have influenced the development of moral theology in the United States in the twenty-year period following the close of Vatican Council II. Change and development will always create some tensions. In the discipline of moral theology these tensions arise not only with respect to the discipline of moral theology itself but also with respect to the Catholic Church and the teaching roles and functions within the church. Contemporary moral theology not only employs somewhat new and different methodologies, but it also at times comes to conclusions that are different from those proposed by official hierarchical church teaching. These tensions within the church caused by recent developments in moral theology are also discussed in the second chapter.

Chapter three explains my approach to the question of what is distinctive and unique about Christian ethics and Christian morality. This question has frequently been debated in the contemporary literature but is closely related with a perennial question for Christian morality and Christian ethics — what is the relationship between the Christian and the human. A final chapter in this section shows how moral theology has developed in responding to one of the more significant developments of the contemporary world, the great strides that have been made in biomedicine.

"Part Two: Moral Theology Looks at Our Society" considers in five different chapters some important issues facing our society — just taxation, filial and societal fiscal responsibility for the elderly, human rights, the United States economy, and the difference between personal morality and public policy. In the process of discussing such significant issues these chapters also develop the basic perspectives and principles which should form the approach to these questions — the nature, function, and role of the state; the three types of justice —

commutative, distributive, and legal or social justice — which govern human relationships in this world; human rights including both political and economic rights; the preferential option for the poor; and the universal destiny of the goods of creation to serve the needs of all. Historical consciousness also comes to the fore in the recognition of how the Catholic tradition has developed over the years in dealing with these important concepts and issues.

The ecclesial aspects of moral theology are also apparent in this second part of the book. The social mission of the church is a constitutive dimension of its one mission of preaching the gospel and working for the redemption of humankind. However, questions arise as to how the church should carry out its social mission. The eighth chapter addresses some aspects of this question in discussing the pastoral letter on the United States economy. Ecclesiology is also intimately linked to social ethics by the statement in the 1971 Synod of Bishops that if the church is to speak credibly to the world about justice, the church itself must be just. The seventh chapter touches on this aspect in its discussion of human rights in society and in the church.

Thus the chapters gathered together in this book attempt to present a better understanding of both the discipline of moral theology as it exists today with emphasis on the context in the United States and at the same time to show how the evolving Catholic tradition of social ethics and the church itself should address some of the significant questions facing our society.

This book is dedicated to all those people at The Catholic University of America who have supported me in my role as a Catholic theologian. In addition I owe a debt of gratitude to those who helped more specifically in the work of preparing this volume. I am particularly grateful to Donnalee Kulhawy and Bonnie Gould who typed this manuscript and have most generously helped me in responding to a huge correspondence in the last years. This book also gives me the occasion to thank publicly C. Gerard Austin, who has served for three years as chair of the Department of Theology at The Catholic University of America, and Johann Klodzen, the ad-

ministrative assistant of the department. The library staff of
Mullen Library at The Catholic University of America have
continued to be most obliging and helpful — especially Bruce
Miller, David Gilson, and Mary Liu, as well as Carolyn Lee.
John Ehmann, my editor at the University of Notre Dame
Press, has assisted me in many ways. Kevin Forrester pre-
pared the index.

I gratefully acknowledge the permission of the following
publishers and periodicals to republish materials which first
appeared in their publications: The Westminster Press, for
"The Historical Development of Moral Theology," which
originally appeared in the *Westminster Dictionary of Christian
Ethics; Le Supplément*, for "Moral Theology in the United States:
An Analysis of the Last Twenty Years"; *The Annual of the Society
of Christian Ethics*, for "What Is Distinctive and Unique about
Christian Ethics and Christian Morality?"; *Studia Moralia*, for
"Moral Theology in Dialogue with Biomedicine and Bioethics";
The Journal of Religious Ethics, for "Just Taxation in the Roman
Catholic Tradition"; *Social Thought,* for "Filial Responsibility
for an Elderly Parent"; Ecumenical Press and Hippocrene
Books, for "Religious Freedom and Human Rights in the
World and in the Church: A Christian Perspective," which
originally appeared in Leonard Swidler, ed., *Religious Liberty
and Human Rights in Nations and Religions*; Macmillian Publishing Company, for "An Analysis of the United States Bishops'
Pastoral Letter on the Economy," which originally appeared
in Thomas M. Gannon, ed., *The Catholic Challenge to the American Economy;* Sheed and Ward, for "The Difference between
Personal Morality and Public Policy," which originally appeared in Madonna Kolbenschlag, ed., *Authority, Community
and Conflict.*

Moral Theology Looks at Itself

1: The Historical Development of Moral Theology

The opening studies collected in this book deal with the discipline of moral theology as such. To understand, analyze, and criticize what is happening in moral theology today, it is helpful to examine how moral theology has developed historically to its present state. This chapter will study this historical development, including an overview of what is happening on the contemporary scene.

I. The Manuals of Moral Theology

Catholic moral theology as a separate discipline distinct from all other theology came into existence at the end of the sixteenth and the beginning of the seventeenth centuries. In Thomas Aquinas' (d. 1274) *Summa theologiae* there was no separate discipline of moral theology, but reflection on moral life was connected in a systematic and integral way with the one theology. After Aquinas the influence of nominalism with its emphasis on the individual and the uniqueness of every moral choice negatively affected all systematic theology.

At the time of the Reformation there were two significant strands in what would be called today moral theology. A Thomistic revival in the fifteenth-century university world made the *Summa* the primary text. Commentaries on the *Secunda pars* of the *Summa*, which deals with the moral life of the Christian and its virtues, were the primary form of publication. Thomas de Vio, later Cardinal Cajetan (d. 1534), Francis de Vitoria (d. 1546), who contributed so much to international law, and the somewhat later Dominican school of Salamanca illustrate such an approach in the sixteenth century. The Jesuits Gabriel Vasquez (d. 1604) and Francis Suarez (d. 1617) were also well-known commentators of the *Summa*. At the same time there also existed *Summae confessariorum* that had begun to appear in the thirteenth century. These were very practical books, often arranged in alphabetical order with little or no abstract reasoning, which dealt in a very positivistic way with the considerations of the moral life.

One of the first theological responses to the Reformation took the form of an apologetic in defense of the Catholic faith. Robert Bellarmine's (d. 1621) *Disputationes de controversiis* well illustrates such a genre. Bellarmine considered all theological issues, including those which might be thought of as pertaining to moral theology—free will, sin, vows, sacrament, merit, etc. His whole approach was apologetic rather than systematic, and obviously polemical.

In the beginning of the Counter-Reformation period an important new genre came into existence—the *Institutiones theologiae moralis*, which continued as the manuals or textbooks for moral theology until Vatican Council II. As part of the attempt to reform Catholic life and institutions the Council of Trent stressed the importance of the sacrament of penance and decreed that all Catholics in the state of grave sin were obliged to confess once a year to the priest according to the number and species of their sins. To accomplish this reform it was necessary to train priests as confessors for the sacrament of penance, with special attention given to the role of the confessor as a judge of the existence and the gravity of sinful acts. In this connection the *Ratio studiorum* of the Society of Jesus proposed a special two-year course to train future priests that would begin with a brief treatment of the principles of fundamental moral theology (the end of human existence, human acts, the moral law, sin), then discuss the moral life of the Christian on the basis of the ten commandments, and finally treat the sacraments especially in the light of how they were to be administered and celebrated. John Azor (d. 1603), a Jesuit theologian teaching in Rome, followed this approach and published his class notes under the title of *Institutiones theologiae moralis*. The world of Catholic theology after

university → *seminary*
(over for morality / morality)

Trent shifted from a university base to a seminary setting in which the professional training of future priests became the primary purpose. In this context the genre of the *Institutiones theologiae moralis* quickly spread. The method and tone of these manuals became generally accepted as the proper approach to moral theology within the Roman Catholic tradition until very recently.

Moral theology in this context was removed from the influence of sacred scripture, dogmatic theology, and spiritual theology and became closely allied with canon law. This discipline was primarily interested, not in speculative or systematic concerns, but in the practical concern of judging if a particular action were sinful or not and the degree of sinfulness. Vital concerns in moral theology such as character development and the virtues of the acting person were skipped over. The tone of these manuals was legalistic, extrinsic, and minimalistic as they dealt with their basic concern of whether or not particular actions were right or wrong on the basis of their conformity to the law of God principally seen in terms of the ten commandments and the laws of the church.

morality allied w/ canon law

In the seventeenth and eighteenth centuries a sharp controversy arose in moral theology between laxists and rigorists that centered on what was later called the moral systems. Doubtlessly some of the manualists in the seventeenth century fell into laxism, for example, Antonine of Diana, Anthony Escobar, Thomas Tamburini, and John Caramuel, a Cistercian monk who was later called "the prince of laxists." Extreme reaction against the laxists arose mainly among the Jansenists in France and took the form of rigorism in the writings of Anthony Arnauld, Peter Nicole, and Blaise Paschal. Often the Jesuits as a whole were accused of laxism, but such a charge is not true. These controversies were quite heated and evoked strong reactions on the part of many. In 1679 the Holy Office under Pope Innocent XI condemned 65 propositions associated with laxism. Among laxist positions condemned as at least scandalous and dangerous in practice were the following: it is sufficient to make an act of faith only once in a lifetime; we are able to satisfy the precepts of loving our neighbor only by external acts. In 1690 Pope Alexander VIII condemned some extreme rigorist positions, for example, those who do not have the most pure love of God uncontaminated in any way are to be excluded from the eucharist.

Much of the debate centered on what was later called the moral systems — how does one move from theoretical doubt about the existence of a law or obligation to the practical certitude necessary to act. The one extreme of absolute tutiorism maintained that in doubt one had to follow the safer course, that is, the existence of a duty, law, or obligation. The opposite extreme of laxism held that one could follow an opinion in favor of freedom from the law even if the arguments in its favor were only tenuously probable (the Latin word really means proveable) or even much less probable than the arguments in favor of the obligation. Both of these extremes were condemned by the above-mentioned papal interventions, but the debate continued. After 1656 the Dominicans generally proposed a probabiliorism according to which one could follow the opinion for freedom from the law only if it were more probable than the opinion in favor of the law or obligation. The Jesuits were generally supporters of a probabilism according to which one could follow the opinion for freedom from the law provided it was probable, or, as often phrased, truly or solidly probable. Unfortunately the discussions often degenerated into polemics.

After the suppression of the Jesuits, Alphonsus Liguori (d. 1787) became the leading defender of a moderate probabilism that was attacked by the Dominicans Concina and Patuzzi. Alphonsus, who was the founder of the Redemptorist order, called his theory equiprobabilism — one could follow the opinion in favor of freedom from the law if it were equally as probable as the opinion for the law. Perhaps the greatest reason for the ultimate success of Alphonsus was the prudential way in which he approached all moral problems and offered his solutions. Later popes declared him a saint, a doctor of the church, and the patron of moral theologians and confessors. Although Alphonsus wrote much on spiritual and ascetical theology, his manual of moral theology followed the general method and outline of the *Institutiones*.

Modern Catholic moral theology until the time of Vatican

Council II (1962-1965) was practically identified with the manuals of moral theology. These textbooks employed a natural law methodology and had the primary purpose of preparing priests for the role of confessors in the sacrament of penance. Their orientation was pragmatic and casuistic, with the ultimate goal of determining what was sinful and what was the gravity of the sin. The manuals often consisted of three volumes. The first volume of fundamental moral theology discussed the ultimate end of human beings, human acts, law as the objective norm of morality, conscience as the subjective norm of morality, sin, and virtue. The second volume treated the morality of specific actions, with the Jesuit and Redemptorist manuals following the format of the ten commandments, whereas the Dominican authors organized their approach on the basis of the virtues. The third volume considered the moral obligations arising from the celebration and reception of the sacraments and was heavily based on the requirements of canon law.

Some changes began to appear in Germany even in the nineteenth century. The Tübingen School started with the pioneering work of John Michael Sailer (d. 1832), who attempted a systematic presentation of the ideal of the Christian way that all are called to follow. John Baptist Hirscher (d. 1865) based his moral theology on the biblical concept of the Kingdom of God. The approach of the Tübingen School continued to have some effect, especially in the work of Fritz Tillmann (d. 1953).

In the midtwentieth century especially in France (e.g., Th. Deman) the neo-Thomist movement stressed an intrinsic, intellectualistic, and realistic understanding of natural law as the basis for moral theology as distinguished from the extrinsic, voluntaristic, and nominalistic method of the manuals. This Thomistic renewal insisted that the good is the primary ethical category, for something is commanded because it is good. Too often the impression was given by existing manuals that something was good because it was commanded. This Thomistic approach also insisted on the importance of the virtues and rejected the legal model of most manuals.

These various reforming trends in Catholic moral theology

continued to grow somewhat before and after the Second World War, but the manuals of moral theology remained entrenched as the basic way of understanding and teaching moral theology. The most significant work in the revival of moral theology in the twentieth century was Bernard Häring's *The Law of Christ*, published originally in Germany in 1954 as a 1146-page volume that later went through many different editions and has been translated into more than fifteen modern languages. Häring, a German Redemptorist, followed in the footsteps of the Tübingen School but also did not neglect many of the concerns of the manuals of moral theology. He gave heavy emphasis to the scriptures and saw all the moral life in terms of the believer's response to the gracious gift of God in Christ. *The Law of Christ* did not overlook a consideration of the morality of particular acts, but it stressed the importance of the person and the growth of the person through continual conversion. Häring attempted to relate moral theology to the broader concerns of scripture, systematic theology, and liturgy. At the same time his philosophical understanding rested heavily on the phenomenology of Max Scheler. In addition to Häring, Josef Fuchs and Gerard Gilleman contributed to the renewal of Catholic moral theology in the pre-Vatican II period.

II. Moral Theology After Vatican II

There can be no doubt that great changes have occurred in Catholic moral theology since Vatican II (1965). The rest of the chapter will summarize these developments, but two cautions are in order. First, Vatican II represents a significant turning point, but the council must be seen in its proper historical context. New developments in scripture, theology, liturgy, and catechetics had already begun to appear in Catholic life and thought before Vatican II, and the council gave authoritative and official approval to these.

A second caution recognizes that while change has taken place in the last few decades in Catholic moral theology, there has also been great continuity as well. The most distinctive characteristic of Catholic moral theology has been its insistence on a mediation that has often been expressed by the Catholic insistence on the "and"—scripture *and* tradition; faith *and* reason; grace *and* nature; Jesus *and* the church; faith *and* works. Distortions have arisen at times in the past by giving too independent a role to the second element in the couplet. Contemporary Catholic theology in continuity with its own tradition has held on to the second elements but now sees them in closer relationship with and even dependent upon the first. Traditional Catholic natural law theory well illustrates this emphasis on mediation. To determine what is to be done, one does not go immediately to God and God's will or plan, but rather the plan of God is discovered by human reason reflecting on human nature. Contemporary Catholic moral theology continues to insist on the role of reason and the human but now tries to understand it in a more integral way in the light of a total faith perspective. This basic insistence on mediation continues to characterize Catholic moral theology.

Developments have occurred in Catholic moral theology in the following areas: the role of scriptures, the relationship to all theology, the philosophical underpinnings, the scope and purpose of moral theology, and a broader emphasis on dialogue in general.

Role of the Scriptures

The papal encyclical *Divino afflante spiritu* in 1943 cautiously opened the door for Catholic exegetes to employ a critical method in understanding the scriptures. Vatican II continued this direction and affirmed the primary role of the scriptures in all theology. The Decree on Priestly Formation of Vatican II (n. 16) specified that the scientific exposition of moral theology should be more thoroughly nourished by scriptural teaching.

The recognition of the scriptures as the "soul of all theology" had significant repercussions on moral theology. Morality is seen above all as a religious morality—as response to the gift and call of God. The emphasis from the scriptures also argues against the Pelagianism, or danger of works righteousness, that was a perennial temptation in Catholic thought. Above all a scripture-oriented method changes the whole scope of moral theology, which could no longer be principally oriented to train confessors as judges in the sacrament of penance. A life-centered moral theology shows the need for the Christian to respond ever more fully to the gracious gift of God in Christ Jesus. The work of Bernard Häring best illustrates such a biblically based approach to moral theology.

However, the discipline of moral theology is also conscious of the limitations in the use of the scriptures. The Catholic tradition has always recognized the place of tradition and of reason in ethics, but now theologians appreciate the need to put all these elements into a more integrated whole.

The limitations of the scriptures appear especially in the hermeneutical question of going from the time and circumstances in which the scriptures were written to the different historical and cultural realities of our age. There is a consensus that the scriptures play a more significant role in the more general aspects of moral theology such as the dispositions of the person and the important values present in social life but a lesser role on particular questions more influenced by changing historical and cultural circumstances. The scriptures cannot be used as a proof text for a very specific moral conclusion which is often arrived at on other grounds. The recognition of the fundamental importance but also the limitations of the scriptures in moral theology calls for a more adequate understanding of exactly how the scriptures should be used in moral theology.

Relationship to All Theology

Moral theology has become more integrated into the whole of theology. Perhaps the most significant change occurred in understanding the relationship between the natural and the supernatural. Previously the Catholic tradition often understood the supernatural as a realm above the natural, a view that H. Richard Niebuhr described as a Christ-above-culture model. Life in the world was under the guidance of the natural law, whereas those who wished to follow the gospel left the world and entered the religious life. Vatican II recognized that both faith and the scriptures had to be related ever more intimately to daily life in the world. Theologians, especially Karl Rahner, have overcome the supernatural-natural duality on the grounds that nature is at best a remainder concept in Catholic theology. Pure nature as such has never existed. The remainder concept is an abstract reality to prove that God's gift of sharing in the fullness of God's grace is sheer gift and not due to us as human beings. Nature as such has never existed. All human beings have been created to share in the fullness of God's love. The older duality and extrinsic relationship between the realm of the supernatural and the realm of the natural can no longer be accepted.

However, in overcoming the theological dualism between the realm of the supernatural and the realm of the natural and by insisting on the fact that the gospel must be relevant to daily life, there arose the danger of an overly optimistic theology which forgets the realities of finitude, sin, and the fullness of the eschaton as future. As in much of Christian theology, an eschatology which recognizes the tension between the now and the not yet has become prominent in contemporary Catholic moral theology. Thus from a theological perspective the most significant change in post-Vatican II moral theology is the overcoming of the dualism between the realm of the natural and that of the supernatural. However, in keeping with the traditional emphasis on mediation and natural law, as understood from a theological perspective, contemporary Catholic moral theology continues to give great importance to reason and the human as sources of ethical wisdom and knowledge for the Christian as well as for all human beings.

In addition to anthropology and eschatology, contemporary moral theology recognizes the importance of Christology. Systematic theology has begun to emphasize a Christology from below involving an emphasis on Jesus and his life. Political and liberation theologies give great importance to the struggle of Jesus against the forces of oppression and the call for a liberation and salvation that embraces the whole person as well as the social and political structures of human existence.

Contemporary Catholic moral theology also explores much more the relationship between moral theology and liturgy. An emphasis on praxis insists that liturgical and sacramental celebration cannot be divorced from the conditions of daily life. A moral theology that no longer emphasizes the minimal requirements for avoiding sin is more closely connected with spirituality as well as with liturgy.

Philosophical Underpinnings

In pre-Vatican II moral theology the human and human reason were understood in terms of manualistic Scholasticism's approach to natural law. Today a pluralism of different philosophical approaches exists in moral theology.

Three significant criticisms of the older philosophical understanding have been made by revisionist Catholic moral theologians, although these criticisms are rebutted by a minority of contemporary Catholic moralists. First, the shift from classicism to historical consciousness has given greater importance to the particular, the individual, and the changing rather than to the universal, the essential, and the unchanging that were stressed in the older Scholastic understanding. Historical consciousness calls for a more inductive methodology, rejecting the total emphasis on deduction and the logic of the syllogism. Second, there has been a turn to the subject to give greater emphasis to the person and the subject rather than to nature and the object. Perhaps the best illustration of such a change is the significance afforded freedom in contemporary moral theology. Some want to ground all moral theology in the self-transcending subject. Even many (e.g., Ashley-O'Rourke, Wojtyla) who come to the same conclusions as the older Catholic stance still emphasize the personalistic aspect of their understanding. A third criticism accuses the older approach of physicalism in identifying the human moral act with the physical structure of the act and thus condemning contraception or direct killing understood in terms of the physical causality of the act. On this matter a sharp debate continues, with a good number of authors, but not a majority of those writing today, rejecting the charge of physicalism.

A pluralism of philosophical methods now exists in Catholic moral theology. Perhaps the most common of these is a form of transcendental Thomism associated with Karl Rahner and Bernard Lonergan. Phenomenological, linguistic, and pragmatic philosophies also serve as the metaphysical underpinnings of different approaches in contemporary Catholic moral theology. Some political and liberation theologies have emphasized the importance of praxis and of orthopraxis. The insistence on the human and human reason underscores the continuity with the tradition, but now the human and human reason are understood differently.

Life-Centered Moral Theology

In general almost all contemporary moral theologians recognize the need for a life-centered moral theology whose function is not merely to prepare confessors as judges in the sacrament of penance. In some ways this new emphasis can claim continuity with the broader theological tradition in the past and with a Thomistic emphasis on the role of grace and the virtues in moral theology.

The person is both agent and subject. Especially in the light of biblical renewal conversion has been stressed as the fundamental response of the Christian to the call of God. Conversion, or change of heart, makes a disciple of Jesus of one who will then walk in the way of discipleship. From a more philosophical perspective conversion has been seen in the light of Lonergan's understanding of the self-transcending subject.

A very significant development is the concept of fundamental option, which is most often construed in the light of transcendental Thomism. In Thomistic moral theology the basic human choice is that of the ultimate end, and this choice then directs and governs the other particular choices that one makes. One either loves God above things and directs all other actions to that end or one chooses a creature, ultimately oneself, as the last end and directs all other actions to that end. Transcendental Thomism sees the basic option on the level of the subject and of transcendental freedom as distinguished from the level of the object and of categorical freedom. In every categorical act (e.g., walking, praying, lying) there is also present the I who performs the act. The fundamental option, or the relationship with God, is on the level of transcendental freedom. The subject is related to God not as object but as the absolute horizon of human reality. This basic actuation or option of the person is known in a transcendental and direct, nonreflex manner in contrast to the reflex conceptual knowledge one has of objects and of particular categorical acts. The concept of fundamental option as the basic orientation of the person can then serve as the philosophical starting point for a more positive and dynamic moral theology. At the present state of the discipline such systematic developments remain inchoate and tentative.

Most often the concept of fundamental option has been used to understand better the traditional concept of mortal sin as involving a changing of the fundamental option away from union with God. Such a change in fundamental option usually occurs as the result of a process and obviously cannot be judged merely on the basis of the categorical act alone. A categorical act may be called right or wrong, but it alone cannot be an adequate criterion for judging if there has been a change in the fundamental option. In an older approach mortal sin as a serious act against the law of God was considered to be a somewhat common occurrence. Mortal sin understood as a fundamental option will occur much less frequently in Christian existence.

The emphasis on the person in moral theology has focused great attention on growth and development in the moral life. Such growth is often understood in terms of a continual conversion that has both scriptural and philosophical roots. Moral theology has also been in critical dialogue with psychological theories of growth as espoused by Piaget, Erickson, Kohlberg, Gilligan, and others.

With a greater emphasis given to the person, character and virtue have again become important topics in moral theology. Contemporary approaches to virtue usually abandon the Thomistic concept of the cardinal virtues and the faculty psychology on which they were based. There have been no systematic approaches to the whole question of the virtues and to the development of a moral theology on the basis of the virtues, but individual virtues such as hope and truthfulness as well as justice and peace have been stressed. The importance of the person as agent and subject has brought about the linking of moral theology with spiritual theology, liturgy, and sacramental theology. The emphasis on narrative in contemporary theology finds its most appropriate application in moral theology in terms of the attitudes, character, and dispositions of the person.

Some, however, have pointed out the danger that in giving great importance to the subject one might fail to recognize the social, political, and cosmic dimensions of the Christian life. Catholic ecclesiology and the Catholic theological tradition in general have consistently recognized the communal and social dimensions of human existence. The eschatology described above also underscores the political and social dimensions of Christian life in this world. These emphases have frequently been invoked to avoid the danger of an overemphasis on the subject.

The Dialogical Nature of Contemporary Moral Theology

Perhaps the most significant characteristic of the entire work of Vatican II was the emphasis on dialogue. Dialogue also adequately describes what is occurring in contemporary Catholic moral theology, above all an ecumenical dialogue with other Christians. Such a dialogue has brought about significant convergences in Protestant and Roman Catholic moral theology. Also a dialogue with contemporary philosophies has resulted in Scholastic philosophy no longer serving as the monolithic philosophical basis of contemporary Catholic moral theology. A dialogue with the sciences has been encouraged by a more inductive methodology with its emphasis on the signs of the times. Official church documents now recognize the need to dialogue with all people of good will.

Further Changes and Disagreements

One cannot doubt that very significant changes have occurred in Catholic moral theology since Vatican II. Since these changes have only recently come to the surface, few systematic approaches to moral theology have developed in the light of new tendencies. The extent and diversity of the changes point to a methodological pluralism in moral theology today, but this pluralism also includes updated modifications of the methodology of the manuals.

These methodological shifts logically involve significant changes on specific substantive issues. Without doubt the controversy over artificial contraception was the most significant single substantive issue in the Catholic Church since Vatican II. In the 1960s some Catholic theologians gingerly suggested the possibility of change in the official Catholic condemnation of artificial contraception for married couples. The pope announced the existence of a commission to study the question. More theologians began to argue for a change, but Pope Paul VI on July 29, 1968, issued the encyclical *Humanae vitae* which reiterated the condemnation of artificial contraception. Continued discussion of this particular issue merged with newer developments in methodology, and the revisionist approach to Catholic moral theology grew. Many revisionist approaches also questioned other accepted teachings of the Catholic Church in the areas of personal, sexual, and medical morality. However, in all these areas the official teaching of the Catholic Church has remained the same.

Methodological and some substantive changes have also occurred in the area of social and political ethics, as liberation theologies involving women, the poor, and blacks, the acceptance of religious liberty, a greater stress on the communal aspect of the goods of creation as existing to serve the needs of all, the possibility of dialogue between Catholics and Marxists, the acceptance of pacifism as a legitimate option for the individual. Many of these changes in the area of social ethics have been accepted by official church teaching.

However, there has also been opposition to the methodological and substantive changes which have occurred. In all parts of the world some Catholic moral theologians staunchly disagree with the newer methodological approaches by either defending the manualistic natural law methodology or by modifying such approaches but still supporting the official teaching of the church on specific controversial questions such as contraception.

It is impossible to chronicle all the areas of debate in contemporary Catholic moral theology, but three significant disputes stand out — the existence of a unique Christian morality, the question of universal moral norms, and the possibility of dissent from official church teaching.

On the methodological level the question of the relationship between Christian ethics and human ethics has been raised. Many contemporary moral theologians maintain there is no unique material content to Christian morality in terms of norms and proximate goals, attitudes, and dispositions. History and experience seem to point out that non-Christians often in theory and in practice recognize attitudes and actions that sometimes have been thought to be uniquely Christian such as self-sacrificing love or reconciliation. A theological acceptance of the fact that all people are offered the gift of salvation also tends to downplay differences between Christians and others that would be based on the presence or absence of saving grace. Proponents of this position cite Thomas Aquinas in their favor and maintain that Catholic moral theology has seen the Christian not in opposition to the human but in bringing the human to its fullest perfection. In this view the specifically Christian or uniquely Christian affects the levels of the transcendental aspects of the Christian life. The other position maintains that faith, grace, and Jesus Christ should have some unique effect on the Christian and how Christians act. At the very least some insist that Christianity brings with it specific individual calls to particular people especially in terms of all the different vocations within the Christian community. In Germany the debate has taken place between the proponents of an autonomous morality and those who advance an ethic of faith, with the latter proposing faith's distinctive contribution to morality. Differences in approaches to this question often result in important methodological differences of grounding moral theology in experience or in revelation. However, even those who deny a unique content to Christian morality recognize that a Christian moral theology must reflect on moral experience in the light of the specifically and distinctively Christian understandings and symbols. At the same time those who hold to a unique Christian content or morality also recognize that there is much in common with all human beings. Chapter three will develop in greater detail my approach to this question.

Perhaps the most divisive debate in contemporary Catholic moral theology concerns the existence of universally binding norms and their grounding. The practical and pastoral implications of this debate emphasize its significance for the daily life of the church. The Scholastic moral theology of the manuals held that certain acts were intrinsically evil on the basis of the object of the act itself independent of intention, circumstances, and consequences. The debate often centered in the middle and late 1960s on the particular question of contraception but soon expanded to other areas in which the human or moral dimension of the act was identified totally with the physical structure of the act. Revisionists maintain that the evil in acts such as contraception, sterilization, or even direct killing is not moral evil but physical, ontic, or premoral evil that can be justified for a proportionate reason. In subsequent discussion proportionalists have attempted to refute the charge that their position leads to sheer consequentialism and utilitarianism.

A most significant debate in contemporary moral theology centers on the teaching function of the hierarchical magisterium and the legitimacy of dissent from authoritative, noninfallible church teaching on specific moral issues. All Christians recognize a general teaching function of the church in moral matters. Catholics accept the hierarchical teaching office committed to the pope and bishops, but there are different ways of understanding this teaching office and how it functions. Technically speaking, the question of dissent in the area of moral theology deals with the authoritative, noninfallible church teaching on specific questions such as contraception, sterilization, direct killing, and such. Only a small minority holds that any of these questions involve the infallible teaching office of the church. Those admitting the possibility of dissent both by theologians and by the faithful argue on a number of grounds. Ecclesiologically, the total teaching function of the church is not exhausted by the hierarchical teaching office and function. Theologically, these specific moral questions are not core and central to the faith, so that in disagreeing with them one is not denying faith. Epistemologically, on such complex specific questions one can never achieve a certitude that excludes the possibility of error. Those arguing against dissent stress the presence of the Spirit to be with the official teachers of the church, so that the faithful can have confidence in following their teaching in difficult matters. Some would recognize an occasional possibility of dissent but not the broad possibility of dissent posed by many contemporary revisionists. The revisionist position logically recognizes not only a pluralism with regard to methodologies existing in contemporary Roman Catholicism but also the possibility of pluralism with regard to specific moral questions where the hierarchical magisterium has already spoken.

This first study has attempted to situate contemporary Catholic moral theology in the light of its historical development and to give an overview of what is happening in moral theology at the present time. Subsequent chapters in this first part will examine in greater depth some of the more significant developments in contemporary Catholic moral theology.

2: Moral Theology in the United States: An Analysis of the Last Twenty Years

To analyze the development of moral theology in the United States in the twenty years since the end of the Second Vatican Council is no simple task. To facilitate such a study this chapter will consider the contexts of Catholic moral theology in the United States, will give a brief overview of its content, and will conclude with an analysis of the tensions in the church created by these developments. The context within which moral theology is done obviously has a great influence on the approach and the very content of moral theology. There are four important contexts of moral theology in the United States that help to explain what has happened in the last twenty years — the ecclesial, the societal, the ecumenical, and the academic.

I. The Contexts of Moral Theology

Ecclesial Context

Since moral theology like all theology is in the service of the church, it is only natural that what happens in the life of the church will have a significant impact on moral theology. The Second Vatican Council and its aftermath have had a great influence on Catholic moral theology throughout the world and in the United States.

In general, moral theology in the United States was unaware of the renewal of moral theology that was brought to a head by the Second Vatican Council. There were no leading

20

figures in moral theology in the United States at the time who were really calling for a change in the basic orientation and method of the discipline. The primary purpose in teaching moral theology was to train confessors for the sacrament of penance, especially in terms of the role of judge, and the method of the manuals of moral theology was generally followed.

The renewal of moral theology that began in Europe and was encouraged by Vatican II called for both a new orientation and a somewhat different methodology. Moral theology could no longer view its function primarily as training priests to be confessors in the sacrament of penance. Within the context of this narrow orientation moral theology was basically interested in determining what was sinful and the degree of sinfulness involved in particular acts. The renewal of moral theology called for a life-oriented moral theology that reflects on the totality of the Christian life, including the gospel call to perfection and holiness. The newer methodological approach above all stressed the important role of the scriptures, the need to overcome the gulf between faith and daily life, as well as between the supernatural and the natural, the importance of historicity, and the necessity for moral theology to be in dialogue with other theological disciplines.

One of the first and most significant consequences of the renewal in moral theology was the fact that the leading moral theologians in the United States before the council were not prepared to deal well with the newer developments in orientation and methodology. As a result the leadership in post-Vatican II moral theology in the United States passed to a new group of younger theologians who were just beginning to teach moral theology in the 1960s. Throughout the period after the council there were no real leaders in Catholic moral theology who had been in the field for a great number of years. The generation teaching moral theology before the council generally found it very difficult to adapt to the changes brought about by the renewal, and many of them withdrew from the field of moral theology.

Moral theology in the United States could not avoid the practical issues which confronted the church in this period.

The North American penchant for dealing with practical problems also influenced moral theology in this country. The most significant issue in the early post-Vatican II period was that of artificial contraception for married couples.

At the time a number of revisionist theologians were calling for a change in the teaching on artificial contraception, and a great many disagreed with the conclusions of the 1968 encyclical *Humanae vitae* condemning this practice. The revisionist theologians appealed to newer insights found in Vatican II and in the renewal of moral theology to support their position. Historical consciousness was a very important concept for revisionist theologians. It is fair to say that in general the United States made little or no contribution to the theology of Vatican II except in the area of religious liberty. John Courtney Murray's work had been a major, if not the major, influence on the new teaching on religious freedom proposed at Vatican II. The American Jesuit appealed above all to historical consciousness to argue for the need to change the older condemnation of religious liberty and to justify the fact that such change could be understood in terms of a true development.[1] In the same way many moral theologians maintained that changed circumstances and changing knowledge in the biological and medical area called for a change in the teaching on artificial contraception. Revisionist theologians also appealed to the renewal of moral theology to put greater stress on the person and the subject rather than on human nature. Personalism and historical consciousness called for a change in the old understanding of natural law, especially as applied to artificial contraception and other issues of sexuality.[2]

After *Humanae vitae* the moral question of artificial contraception became intimately involved with the ecclesiological issue of the teaching role of the hierarchical magisterium and the proper response of the faithful. In theory and practice revisionist Catholic theologians have accepted the possibility of responsible dissent from authoritative, authentic, noninfallible hierarchical teaching. Again the revisionists appealed to a changing understanding of the church proposed in Vatican II to justify the possibility of dissent. The church is the whole people of God. An older absolute division between the *ecclesia* docens and the *ecclesia discens* can no longer be accepted. The noninfallible teaching of the hierarchical magisterium on specific moral issues cannot claim to have absolute certitude. One can speak of a presumption in favor of this teaching, but the presumption always cedes to the truth. Again the appeal to historical consciousness calls for a hermeneutic, or interpretation, of past formulations of hierarchical teaching.

However, a minority of moral theologians defended the teaching of *Humanae vitae* and strongly opposed at least in practice the possibility of dissent from such teaching. Germain Grisez, who was trained in philosophy, published in 1964 a defense of the official teaching on contraception that in its own way involved a revision of the accepted Catholic arguments against artificial contraception.[3] Grisez rejects the argument from a conventional natural law approach that contraception is intrinsically immoral because by it one engaging in intercourse prevents the act from attaining its natural end. The natural teleology of human functions does not necessarily require absolute moral respect.[4] Grisez also denies the validity of the phenomenological argument against artificial contraception based on sexual intercourse as an experience of love as a total giving because it is connected with a very questionable philosophical theory of human beings and of the marital society.[5] In opposition to conventional natural law theory and situationism Grisez develops his own theory of practical principles based on the moral obligation never to go against essential or basic human goods. In subsequent years Grisez has further elaborated his fundamental theory. Grisez also holds that the teaching condemning artificial contraception is infallibly proposed by the ordinary magisterium.[6]

The lively debates sparked by *Humanae vitae* in 1968 heavily influenced the course of moral theology in the United States and in the world. The two questions of the existence of absolute norms and the proper response to the noninfallible hierarchical church teaching have dominated the concerns of moral theology since that time.

There can be no doubt that a strong division exists among United States' theologians in general and moral theologians in particular on these two issues that are very closely intertwined. Most Catholic theologians in the United States belonged to the Catholic Theological Society of America that came into existence in 1946. Until the late 1960s this was a clerical organization consisting mostly of seminary professors. However, the complexion of the membership began to change in the late 60s, and many of the older members no longer attended the meetings. In 1955 the first national meeting of the Society of Catholic College Teachers of Sacred Doctrine was held with the purpose of strengthening the teaching of theology in Catholic colleges. Later this society changed its name to the College Theology Society and became ecumenical, but it still remains a predominately Catholic group.[7]

The vast majority of the membership of these two academic societies became generally associated in the 70s with the revisionist and progressive trends in Catholic theology, although obviously all the members did not accept these positions. Perhaps the most publicized illustration of this development was the publication in 1977 of *Human Sexuality: New Directions in United States Catholic Thought*.[8] This volume was actually the report of a committee established by the Board of Directors of the Catholic Theological Society of America in 1972. The committee report like all other previous reports was received by the Board of Directors and never actually approved by the board or by the membership at large. *Human Sexuality* evoked a significant debate, thus fulfilling one of its intended purposes. The methodological approach and the solution of particular problems proposed in the book were criticized by many revisionists. Although the majority of contributing moral theologians take some revisionist positions, there are differences and debates among them.

To counteract this growing tendency among Roman Catholic theologians and to defend the need for adherence to the hierarchical magisterium a number of more conservative Catholic scholars founded the Fellowship of Catholic Scholars in 1977. Unfortunately the relationships between the two different approaches and the two different groups have not always been cordial and dialogical. These tensions and divisions continue to mark Catholic theology and especially Catholic moral theology in the United States today. In the judgment of some these tensions are often exacerbated by ultraconservative groups and newspapers.[9] However, all concerned should strive for a greater openness to dialogue and mutual respect.

The two questions posed in the wake of the discussion over artificial contraception have continued to be two of the most important concerns addressed by Catholic moral theology in the United States. The issue of the existence and grounding of specific concrete norms has continued to be debated at great length. The revisionist position is often characterized by a proportionalist theory that argues that premoral evil can be done for proportionate reasons.[10] Germain Grisez has tended to be the leading figure in the position upholding the fact that human responsibility means that human beings can never directly go against a basic human good. Such an understanding of responsibility definitely grounds some specific absolute moral norms. In addition, both sides have continued to debate the question of the proper response due by theologians and by the faithful at large to the noninfallible teaching of the hierarchical magisterium. Here revisionist theologians have had support from a good number of ecclesiologists who have generally supported the right to dissent in certain circumstances.

The fact that there exist two generic positions called, for lack of better terms, the conservative and the revisionist, should not hide the fact that there are also many differences within these approaches. In the future it will be beneficial for all concerned to recognize these rather significant differences within each group. Such a recognition will avoid overly simplistic characterizations and should facilitate dialogue and criticism not only between the two groups but also within the two general positions.

Not only the life of the universal church but also the life of the local church has affected moral theology in the United States. Perhaps the most distinctive aspect of this local church influence has been the recent involvement of the American Catholic bishops in social issues especially through their two pastoral letters on peace and the economy. American theologians had been giving some attention to these areas, but the leadership taken by the bishops has focused attention on both issues. As a result, Catholic moral theologians have devoted more attention to these two very significant questions and to the whole area of social ethics. Chapter eight will analyze the pastoral letter of the United States bishops on the economy.

Societal Context

A second important context for moral theology is the societal influence. A number of factors in the United States in the last twenty years have emphasized the importance of ethics. In the 1960s the struggle against poverty, racial discrimination, and war raised the consciousness of the society at large to the importance of ethics. The shock of Watergate in the 1970s only increased the importance of ethical considerations. Questions of law, conscience, and public policy have been discussed at great length. Concern about population growth, energy resources, especially nuclear energy, ecology, and the role of women in society have all contributed to the heightened awareness of the need for ethics.

Within this atmosphere so conducive to the role of ethics a number of significant developments have occurred. Perhaps the most important from the academic perspective has been the interest of philosophy in substantative ethical questions. Until recently this country's philosophical ethics was dominated by the linguistic analysis approach and primarily interested in metaethical questions. But now philosophical journals and books are dealing with all the many ethical questions facing society. Contemporary philosophical work has stimulated moral theology and become an important dialogue partner with moral theology.

Another result of the widespread interest in ethics has been the establishment of different commissions by the government to study problems especially in the area of recent developments in bioethics. The best known and most productive commission is "The President's Commission for the Study of Ethical Problems in Medicine and Biomedical and Behavioral Research," which was active from January 1980 to March 31, 1983. The commission, whose power was only advisory, produced ten reports, five appendix volumes, and a guidebook for institutional review boards. The reports dealt with such topics as defining death, deciding to forego life-sustaining treatment, making health-care decisions, protecting human subjects, screening and counseling for genetic choices, securing access to health care, splicing life, and whistle-blowing in biomedical research.[11] The fourth chapter below will discuss how biomedical developments have affected the discipline of moral theology.

Support for ethical studies has come not only from the government but also from private-sector funding. Think-tanks and research institutions have sprung up to study and assess the ethical aspects of the many different questions facing society. Sometimes theologians, philosophers, and ethicists are part of larger interdisciplinary groups, whereas at other times the institutes tend to be primarily composed of ethicists. This widespread interest in ethics with the resulting growth in institutional support for ethical concerns is a great help to ethics in general, but in my judgment the contribution to moral theology is somewhat ambivalent.

Moral theology and Christian ethics reflect on the moral life in the light of the Christian and Catholic self-understandings. The United States, however, is a pluralistic country in which many people do not share these Christian beliefs. Questions that arise from these differences have both theoretical and practical dimensions. From the theoretical perspective the question concerns whether there exists one moral order which is the same for Christians and for all others or whether there is a unique morality for Christians and another morality for non-Christians. The question has often been addressed in this country in terms of the distinctiveness of Christian ethics and Christian morality. On the basis of both contemporary and traditional Catholic theological insights I maintain there is only one moral order and that the specific content of Christian morality does not differ from what human morality calls for. However, the fact that the explicit material content of Christian morality is *per se* available to all human beings does not mean that moral theology, or Christian ethics, and philosophical ethics are the same. Moral theology explicitly reflects on the Christian life and the one human moral order in the light of explicitly Christian realities.[12] The next chapter will develop my approach to the questions of the uniqueness and distinctiveness of Christian ethics and of Christian morality.

The recognition that the specific moral content is the same, but that moral theology and philosophical ethics are not the same because of their different sources, should guide reaction to what is often happening in the United States today. The American Catholic bishops have recognized in their pastoral letters that they are addressing two different audiences — their fellow believers in the church and the broader public that does not necessarily share their beliefs. In addressing the public at large the pastoral letters prescind from the appeal to specifically Christian sources.[13] Such an approach is certainly legitimate and appropriate.

There exists, however, a danger in some institutes and commissions dealing with public policy. Here the tendency is often to prescind from any Christian sources and to discuss issues in a purely philosophical manner. There is a very apparent problem here for the discipline of moral theology as such. Within such institutes and commissions often there is no room for Christian ethics or Jewish ethics or Muslim ethics. As a result the discipline of moral theology is not helped by such commissions and institutes. At times I can understand why public commissions especially should prescind from religious differences; but, on the other hand, pluralism does not always require that everything should be reduced to the least common denominator. Perhaps even here efforts could be made to show how different religious perceptions can agree but also even disagree on particular issues facing society. The problem is very difficult, but it should be noted that the broad support for ethical institutes and commissions has not necessarily had a positive effect on the development of the discipline of moral theology as such. Chapter four will discuss the impact of the growing discipline of bioethics on moral theology.

The societal context has also brought to the fore the differences between the moral order and the legal order. Catholic moral theology as illustrated in the approach of Thomas Aquinas has always distinguished between the two orders. The emergence of constitutional government, especially as it appeared in the United States with the emphasis given to the freedom of the citizen, has stressed even more the differences between the moral order and the legal order. In my judgment the best approach to this question in theory is found in the principles enshrined in Vatican II's Declaration on Religious Freedom. This document recognizes that the freedom of individuals should be respected as far as possible and curtailed only when and insofar as necessary. Public order with its threefold aspect of justice, peace, and public morality is the criterion that justifies the proper intervention of the state. In addition, laws must be just and enforceable, and also the feasibility of passing such legislation is most significant in supporting possible laws. Unfortunately, it seems that many Catholics in the United States do not consciously realize the practical scope of the difference between the two orders.

In practice, discussions about law and morality have quite frequently occurred in the United States. In the last three presidential elections the question of abortion law has come to the fore in the light of the liberal law now existing in this country. In my judgment the criteria proposed above can justify a more strict law or even the existing law depending on whether one gives more importance to the criterion stressing justice and the need to protect the rights of the innocent or the criteria giving the benefit of the doubt to the freedom of individuals and invoking feasibility. Despite some significant statements to the contrary there is no basis for saying that there is only one Catholic position on the legal aspects of abortion in this country. Chapter nine will analyze in greater depth the distinction between personal morality and public policy.

The role of the United States in the contemporary world has become, especially since the Vietnam era, an important object of discussion and criticism within the society at large. Without a doubt the two most significant questions today involve peace and the economy. Both these issues have important domestic and international aspects, especially in terms of relationships with the third world and with the nations of the southern hemisphere. Catholic ethicists in dialogue with many others of differing backgrounds have been discussing the issues of war and peace. Some Catholic moralists have used the just-war principles in an effort to limit the possible use of nuclear weapons and the arms race. Some have become nuclear pacifists, while a comparatively small but growing and determined group have embraced a total pacifism.[14] As mentioned earlier, the recent pastoral letter of the United States bishops has given a very significant impulse for further study in this area. Catholic moral theologians have given less sustained attention to the issues of economics and the relationship of the United States to the world economic order. Here the American bishops have provided important leadership. The process leading to a pastoral letter on the economy has stimulated much study in this area. Human rights has been an important area of concern both domestically and internationally, and Catholic scholars have been addressing this issue out of the context of the developing Catholic tradition.[15] Chapter seven will examine the Catholic approach to human rights in society at large and in the church.

The role of women in society and feminism have become very significant issues in the United States. Some feminists have declared that Christianity is opposed to feminism and have moved beyond Christianity. Christian feminists strive to show that feminism and Christianity are compatible. Christian feminist ethics is already emerging as a special approach in Christian ethics.[16] There is a growing number of women writing today in the area of moral theology. Feminism is much more than merely a women's issue, but the ever-increasing number of well-trained women theologians will insure that the feminist approach receives its proper place in ethics. Catholic feminists often feel that the institutional church is not open and sympathetic. In practice I think that the most crucial, and unfortunately divisive, issue facing the Catholic Church in the United States is the role of women in church and society. The rightful role and function of women in society and the church is not simply a women's issue but truly a human issue involving human rights and the good of humanity in general, and a Christian issue concerning the community of equal disciples of Jesus.

Ecumenical Context

A third important context for moral theology in the United States is the ecumenical context. This is an entirely new phenomenon that has only emerged in the last twenty years but is very characteristic of the contemporary discipline of moral theology. This ecumenical aspect is now present in such a way that it cannot be dismissed as merely a passing fad.

There are various ways in which the ecumenical emphasis has been institutionalized. There is no society of Catholic moral theologians in the United States. Moral theologians before 1965 belonged almost exclusively to the Catholic Theological Society of America and to the College Theology Society, as it is now called. The Society of Christian Ethics, as it is now called, was founded in 1959 primarily by Protestant seminary professors of Christian social ethics. This society itself has grown considerably from 117 members in 1960-61 to 664 in 1983. In its earliest years the society, which meets once a year and now publishes an annual, was predominantly male, white, and Protestant. Since then there has been a marked increase in the number of female, black, and Roman Catholic members. According to the recently published history of the society, beginning with the year 1965 Roman Catholics began joining the society at the rate of about five or six per year through the 60s. The first Roman Catholic became president of the society in 1971. By 1983 145 Catholics belonged. The programs and the new history of the society bear out the ecumenical aspect of the group.[17]

There are other significant ways in which the ecumenical aspect of moral theology has been institutionalized. Some Catholic moral theologians now teach in denominational, private, and state institutions. A good number of somewhat younger Catholic moral theologians have been trained in and received their degrees from Protestant or independent institutions. The literature in moral theology in the last few years in the United States well illustrates the ecumenical dimension of the discipline. With encouragement from the Society of Christian Ethics and others the *Journal of Religious Ethics* began publishing in 1973 as an independent, ecumenical, academic enterprise dealing with all aspects of religious ethics. The ecumenical character of moral theology is nowhere better illustrated than in the literature reviewed in the "Notes on Moral Theology" that have regularly appeared at least once a year in *Theological Studies*. "Notes on Moral Theology" critically reviews the most important articles that have appeared in the preceding year. Before 1965 the literature reviewed was almost totally Roman Catholic, but now the "Notes" are truly ecumenical without losing their Catholic bases. The contemporary authority, success, and importance of these "Notes" is due to the incisive and penetrating work of Richard A. McCormick, who composed them for nineteen years before passing on the role to others in 1984.

There can be no doubt that the ecumenical aspect has had an impact on Catholic moral theology in the United States, but this has also been a two-way influence, with Catholic ethics also affecting Protestant ethics. One must also remember that the ecumenical dialogue occurs as part of a larger context within which Catholic moral theology is being renewed.

There has been a growing rapprochement between Protestant and Roman Catholic ethics. James M. Gustafson, a University Professor at the University of Chicago and a most respected analyst of Christian ethics, has aided this growing rapprochement in his study of these developments. In the area of practical moral reasoning Protestantism has been consciously moving away from a "wasteland of relativism," whereas Roman Catholics coming from the opposite pole have been searching for responsible openness. To strengthen the discipline Protestantism has been seeking some philosophical base to overcoming the seeming vagaries of historicism and existentialism, whereas Roman Catholics have been revising natural law to overcome its excessive rigidity. From a theological viewpoint Christological concerns and a striving to overcome an extrinsic understanding of nature and grace within the Catholic tradition have brought the two approaches closer together.[18]

Gustafson's analysis is quite accurate, but there is one important aspect missing in his book which the Chicago professor himself has recognized in his study. Gustafson considers only the revisionist moral theologians. The more conservative moral theologians are not mentioned or discussed. As a general rule it is true that the ecumenical aspect is more pronounced among revisionist Catholics than among the more conservative Catholic moral theologians.

However, this general statement must be properly nuanced. A number of more conservative Catholic moral theologians frequently appeal to more conservative Protestants such as Paul Ramsey. Ramsey's positions in medical ethics have often echoed the conclusions of conservative Catholic positions. The *Linacre Quarterly* is the official journal of the National Federation of Catholic Physicians' Guilds, which every year presents its *Linacre Quarterly Award* for the best article that appeared in the journal in the previous year. The 1978 award was presented to Paul Ramsey for his article "Euthanasia and Dying Well Enough" that appeared in the February 1977 issue.[19] It is interesting to note that Ramsey and two other somewhat conservative religious ethicists are members of the editorial advisory board of this journal, but there are no longer any Catholic revisionist moral theologians on the board.

There can be no doubt that especially in areas of sexual and medical ethics Ramsey's conclusions are generally congenial to more conservative Roman Catholics. However, all should recognize that from a methodological viewpoint a great difference exists between Ramsey's approach and traditional Catholic emphases. Ramsey adopts a deontological methodology based on faithful, covenant love. The Thomistic tradition has an entirely different methodological approach with its emphasis on the ultimate end of human beings and the good. The retired Princeton University professor is strongly opposed to any teleology. It is true that Ramsey has often dealt favorably with the Catholic tradition in areas such as just war and medical ethics, especially the care for the dying. In addition Ramsey has at times spoken favorably about Catholic natural law methodology. However, Ramsey has never really accepted the Catholic concept of natural law. From a theological perspective Ramsey's heavy emphasis on *agape* and his unwillingness to accept the Catholic concept of mediation have always made it somewhat difficult for him to ground theologically any understanding of natural law. From a philosophical viewpoint, even when Ramsey was speaking favorably of Jacques Maritain's approach to natural law, the American Methodist never really accepted the ontological aspect of natural law proposed by the French Thomist. While it is true that Ramsey has dealt extensively with traditional Catholic issues such as just war and ordinary-extraordinary means to preserve life, his treatment of these issues is from his own *agape*-based deontological methodology. Although Ramsey's conclusions are often in agreement with the teachings of the hierarchical magisterium, his methodology considerably differs from traditional Catholic approaches.[20]

In my view the ecumenical dialogue shows the primary differences between Roman Catholic and Protestant ethicists to center on the characteristic Catholic acceptance of mediation. Mediation is distinctive of Catholic theology and is manifested in all aspects of that theology. The revelation of God is mediated through scripture and tradition. The word and work of God are mediated in and through Jesus, and in and through the human instrumentality of the church. The moral call to follow Jesus is mediated in and through the human and human experience. From a theological perspective traditional Catholic natural law theory illustrates the reality of mediation. Catholic ethics appeals, not immediately to the will or word of God, but rather to the human that mediates the divine will and word. It is necessary to remember that one danger in mediation is to absolutize what is only a mediation, and this has often occurred, as exemplified in Catholic ecclesiology.

It is precisely the Catholic insistence on mediation which I see as the critical difference between the Catholic tradition and the theocentric ethics recently proposed by James M. Gustafson. Recall that Gustafson has been quite appreciative of many of the recent developments among Catholic moral theologians. However, his new two-volume study shows again that mediation is often the continuing point of difference between Protestant ethicists of all types and Catholics be they liberal or conservative. Gustafson claims to be following the Reformed tradition in emphasizing the glory of God. The Chicago professor rejects most of contemporary Christian ethics as being too anthropocentric and too much based on the human. God, and not human beings, is the center of meaning. Human fulfillment or human happiness cannot be the primary concern of Christian ethics. Human experience itself underscores the tragic aspects of human existence, and at times human beings must be angry with the God who brings this about. Gustafson also cannot accept the reality of an afterlife.[21] However, in the Catholic tradition there has never been the need to choose between the glory of God and human fulfillment. The glory of God is the human person come alive. The glory of God is seen in and through human fulfillment and happiness. Thus the contemporary dialogue indicates that Protestant and Catholic ethicists often differ over the methodological significance of mediation, whereas Catholics of all different stripes are usually in agreement on this important theological issue.

The analysis given of the ecumenical aspect of moral theology in the United States indicates that the ecumenism involved is a true ecumenism and not just a watering down of one's own Catholic tradition. The integrity of the moral theologians themselves would insure that this is the case. One further illustration of the more substantative differences between Protestant and Catholic ethicists came to the fore in a dispute over abortion occasioned by "A Call to Concern" signed by 209 scholars mostly from the field of Christian ethics and including many well-known Protestant ethicists but noticeably lacking in Catholic support. The document rejected the absolutist position on abortion, supported the 1973 Supreme Court rulings, called for the government to fund abortions for poor people, and expressed sorrow at the heavy institutional involvement of the bishops of the Roman Catholic Church in favor of the absolutist position.[22] It is true that there is a great diversity among Catholic theologians on the question of the legal aspect of abortion and even some diversity on the moral question itself. However, "A Call to Concern" was rejected by the vast majority of Roman Catholic moral theologians. In his recent history of the Society of Christian Ethics Edward LeRoy Long maintains that one of the most valuable meetings in the life of the society involved an honest and frank discussion over "A Call to Concern" at the 1978 meeting.[23]

Academic Context

A fourth significant context of moral theology in the United States is the academic context. For all practical purposes moral theology and all Catholic theology in the United States were not looked on as academic disciplines before the 1960s. Theology was primarily identified with seminary education, which in the pre-Vatican II period meant separation from all other worlds. It is true that theology was taught at all Catholic colleges, but for the most part it was treated as a catechetical rather than an academic enterprise. The professors were usually clerics, many of whom did not have advanced degrees. The very fact of priestly ordination was often judged to be sufficient preparation for teaching theology.

The beginning of the College Theology Society in 1954 indicates an incipient move toward a greater professionalization in the teaching of what was then called sacred doctrine. At the time only priests and brothers were admitted into the Catholic Theological Society of America. Women religious and laity with advanced degrees in theology were looking for a professional organization. This declericalization and continued professionalization of theology began to grow especially in the 1960s. Corresponding to this was the increase in the number of Catholic universities offering a doctorate degree in theology. Theology both in its undergraduate and graduate setting was striving for academic respectability alongside all the other academic disciplines. Vatican II only heightened the interest in and concern for theology as a respected academic discipline in the Catholic college and university.

At the same time the self-understanding of Catholic colleges and universities began to change. Academic freedom had been a hallmark of American higher education throughout its existence. Colleges and universities must be free and autonomous centers of study with no external constraints limiting their autonomy or their freedom.[24] In the post-World War II period Catholic colleges and universities realized that they were more and more a part of American higher education in general. Before 1960 most Catholic educators still thought there was a basic incompatibility between the Catholic institution of higher learning and the American understanding of a college or university with its autonomy and freedom. However, with a growing understanding on the part of American Catholic educators, they realized they should be and could be an integral part of American higher education, and the theological developments highlighted at Vatican Council II also influenced a new approach.[25] The most significant illustration of the new approach was the so-called "Land O' Lakes Statement" issued by 26 leaders in Catholic higher education in the United States and Canada in 1967. The statement makes its point succinctly and forcefully:

> The Catholic university today must be a university in the full modern sense of the word with a strong commitment to and concern for academic excellence. To perform its teaching and research functions effectively, the Catholic university must have a true autonomy and academic freedom in the face of authority of whatever kind, lay or clerical, external to the academic community itself. To say this is simply to assert that institutional autonomy and academic freedom are essential conditions of life and growth and indeed of survival for Catholic universities as for all universities.[26]

The Catholic literature on academic freedom before the 1960s was invariably negative and defensive. However, the middle 1960s saw a growing acceptance of the place for and need of academic freedom in American Catholic higher education. A dissertation accepted at The Catholic University of America in 1969 made the case for the full acceptance of academic freedom for Catholic institutions of higher learning and for Catholic theology,[27] even though a dissertation published in 1958 held the exact opposite position.[28] Perhaps the contemporary scene is best illustrated by the fact that in 1984 a Roman Catholic layman defended a doctoral dissertation "Academic Freedom in the American Roman Catholic University" at Drew University, a graduate school with ties to the Methodist Church![29]

In this context Roman Catholic theology in general and moral theology in particular are looked upon as academic disciplines like other academic disciplines existing within Catholic institutions of higher learning that claim for themselves academic freedom and autonomy. Such a context does not deny anything that is essential to Catholic theology and moral theology as such. Catholic theology can and must recognize the role of the hierarchical teaching office in the church. However, judgments about the competency of Catholic scholars that affect their right to teach in Catholic institutions can only be made by academic peers and not by any authority, clerical or lay, which is external to the academic community itself. Such judgments about competency to teach Catholic theology must give due weight to the teaching of the hierarchical magisterium. The academic freedom of the Catholic institution and of Catholic theology is in the eyes of most United States theologians compatible with a Catholic understanding of the proper role of the hierarchical magisterium and of theologians within the church. Archbishop Weakland of Milwaukee maintains that the acceptance of academic freedom is not merely a compromise with secular reality but makes Catholic institutions of higher learning more effective in their service to the church.[30] A minority of Catholic scholars, in particular those associated with the Fellowship of Catholic Scholars, would not accept such an understanding of academic freedom as applied to Catholic institutions and theology.

The academic context of Catholic theology in the United States means that the theologian cannot see one's role and function in terms of a commissioning to teach given by the hierarchical magisterium in the church. Theology very definitely is in the service of the church, but it is also an academic discipline as such. Recent canonical legislation has been viewed by many as threatening the understanding of theology as an academic discipline and as questioning whether Catholic institutions of higher learning can belong to the mainstream of American higher education.

The academic context of Catholic moral theology comes primarily from the place, the academy, in which theology is done. However, there are different places where theology is being done today. Commissions and think-tanks or institutes have already been mentioned. Very often these institutes are ecumenical and multidisciplinary in their approach. Theologians of various denominations work together with other humanists and scholars in debating the problems facing society and the world. One of the best known of such institutes is the Institute of Society, Ethics, and the Life Sciences, commonly called the Hastings Center, which publishes a very significant journal, *The Hastings Center Report*. Georgetown

University, which is a Catholic institution, houses and sponsors the Kennedy Institute of Ethics, which is ecumenical in
its membership and approach. However, other institutes have
been set up primarily as Catholic centers as such. The best
example of such institutes is the "Pope John XXIII Medical-
Moral Research and Education Center" originally founded
in 1973. This center publishes a newsletter and occasional
books, sponsors workshops, including an annual workshop
for bishops, and arranges meetings for various groups. The
center tends to adopt a more conservative position on the issues
of medical ethics.

In general in the last twenty years the academic aspect of
Catholic theology has been stressed with a resulting strengthening of the position that the Catholic theologian cannot be seen
merely as an extension of the hierarchical teaching office in
the church.

II. Content of Moral Theology

This second section will briefly discuss Catholic moral
theology in the United States from the perspective of the content of moral theology itself. In the light of the very nature
of the discipline as well as the context discussed above, moral
theology will be involved in discussing the major problems
faced by both the church and the society.

The areas of sexual and medical ethics have already been
briefly mentioned. Here the majority of moralists contributing
have adopted a revisionist methodology that argues against
some, but by no means all, of the positions maintained in older
Catholic approaches. According to revisionists the primary
problem of the older methodology is a biologism that identifies the human moral aspects with merely the biological. The
revisionist approach appeals to historical mindedness and personalism to argue against absolute moral norms, in which what
is always forbidden is described in physical or biological terms,
for example, contraception or direct killing. Many maintain
that such physical or premoral evil can be done for a proportionate reason. Especially in the areas of sexual and medical

morality much tension has arisen because here the revisionists propose that one can dissent from the authoritative noninfallible teaching of the hierarchical magisterium. Proponents of the older positions often modify the older natural law arguments but accuse the revisionists of gnosticism in failing to give enough importance to the physical aspects of embodied humanity.

Within the area of social ethics there again exists what is usually called a "conservative-liberal" dispute, but this difference is not exactly the same and does not necessarily involve the same people as the discussion in sexual and medical ethics. In the area of social ethics the American bishops with their earlier statements and especially with their recent pastoral letters on peace and the economy are generally judged to belong to the liberal approach. The more conservative position, as exemplified in a lay letter on the economy as an alternative to the bishops' approach, is much more supportive of the American economic system and more ready to defend the need for a strong nuclear defense policy than are the American bishops.[31] Michael Novak, who is the most prominent and prolific author in this area, proposes a realism which accepts human limitations and sinfulness, rejects utopian solutions, and faults the Catholic tradition for its insistence on distribution rather than on the call to creatively produce more wealth.[32] In this area too there is an ecclesiological discussion, with many of the more conservative authors maintaining that the hierarchical church should not be so specific in its teaching on social issues and should not adopt its generally liberal approach.[33]

How is one to evaluate the consistency of the hierarchical teaching in these two different areas? The United States bishops themselves, under the leadership of Cardinal Bernardin, have been arguing for a consistent life ethic affecting all life issues such as abortion, war, and capital punishment.[34] In general I think there is great merit to such an approach, but there is a tendency to become too unnuanced and to forget the distinction between law and morality.

In my judgment a lack of consistency exists between the positions taken by the American Catholic bishops and the universal hierarchical teaching office in the sexual and medical areas and the approaches taken in social ethics, for two different methodologies appear to be at work in official hierarchical teaching. In the social area official church documents strongly recognize the importance of historical consciousness, and they turn to the subject with an emphasis on the person. These emphases with all their logical conclusions are missing in contemporary hierarchical approaches in the areas of sexual and medical ethics.

In the general area of methodology and fundamental moral theology much work remains to be done. Most attention up to now has been given to the question of norms in moral theology, with Richard A. McCormick doing the most work to develop a theory of proportionalism, while Germain Grisez has strongly defended universal norms with his theory based on an understanding of the modes of responsibility and basic human goods. Speaking as a revisionist, I recognize the need to develop exactly what is meant by proportionate reason and to study all the ramifications of the theory in all aspects and areas of moral theology. Other methodological issues such as the use of scripture in moral theology, the distinctiveness of Christian ethics, and, to a lesser extent, the role of the sciences in moral theology have been discussed.

One fascinating aspect of the ecumenical dialogue has been the recent Protestant emphasis on virtue, character, and the importance of narrative and story, shown especially in the writings of Stanley Hauerwas.[35] As a result Roman Catholics are now much more conscious of what has been such a fundamental aspect of Catholic moral theology but has been generally overlooked in the last few years. However, sustained and systematic studies of the Christian person as agent and subject are needed. Moral development has received quite a bit of attention, especially in dialogue with Kohlberg, Gilligan, and other psychologists. Many articles and even some books have been written on conscience, but much remains to be done. In all these areas of fundamental moral theology one is conscious of the need for interdisciplinary approaches in order to do justice to the anthropological realities involved.

With all the significant changes in the discipline and the manifold specific questions that have emerged, it is natural that there have been few attempts to construct a systematic moral theology. Timothy O'Connell's *Principles for a Catholic Morality*, with its heavy dependence on the work of Joseph Fuchs, deals from a contemporary viewpoint with the issues raised by the older manuals in fundamental moral theology.[36] Daniel Maguire's *The Moral Choice* presents a lively and innovative approach to the specific issue of moral choice.[37] As helpful as these books are, especially for use with students, they are not intended to be systematic studies of all moral theology.

Bernard Häring's three-volume *Free and Faithful in Christ* is really the first attempt at a systematic discussion of contemporary moral theology in a manual-type approach.[38] It is fitting that Häring's book, which was written in English, should be the first attempt at a systematic contemporary moral theology on the American scene. Häring has lectured widely and taught in many different Catholic, Protestant, and state institutions in this country in the past twenty years. It is safe to say that Häring has had a greater influence on the totality of the American Catholic Church than any other moral theologian. Recently Germain Grisez has published *The Way of the Lord Jesus*, vol. 1: *Christian Moral Principles*, a thousand-page treatise that is the first of a projected four-volume systematic moral theology.[39] Grisez here develops again his basic theory of moral responsibility and norms, but he tries to incorporate this within a larger and systematic moral theology.

III. Tensions in the Church

Developments in the past twenty years in the area of moral theology have occurred and brought to the fore many tensions within the Catholic Church. Without uncritically accepting all that has transpired, I favor the revisionist developments that have been briefly described in these last two chapters. The church must be willing to live with a greater pluralism and diversity than have heretofore characterized life in the Catholic Church in this century. However, there are legitimate limits to pluralism.

I reject some of the explanations that have been proposed for what has occurred in contemporary Catholic moral theology. These developments, especially the questions involving dissent, have not been the work of merely a few theologians from any one country. Moral theology is a critical reflection on life, and the experience of Christian people indicates a widespread practical divergence from official church teaching in many areas of human sexuality. Of course, moral theology as a critical and systematic reflection cannot claim that something is right because the majority of people do it. However, the majority of Catholic moral theologians writing in the major European languages have supported in general the recent developments described above. These developments cannot be written off as merely the work of a small group of theologians in one particular country.

Nor can one claim that moral theologians dissent from church teaching on specific moral questions because they are too uncritically accepting of the mores of a materialistic and pagan society. No doubt sin affects all we do, and moral theology must always be critical of contemporary mores. However, in addition the church and theology can and should see in the world the creative and redeeming work of God. It is simplistic and misguided to defend older Catholic teachings on specific issues such as contraception and sterilization as the truths of faith opposed to the evils of the modern world. A critical evaluation following in the footsteps of Vatican II always tries to see in the modern world both the good and the evil.

What are the underlying reasons for the tension existing today between official church teachings and some recent developments in moral theology? It is impossible to discuss all these aspects, but three important realities are the following: historical consciousness, the nature and role of theology, and ecclesiology. In all these areas proponents of the newer tendencies appeal to recent developments in the church, including the teachings of the Second Vatican Council, to support their approach, even though one must also admit the ambiguity found in the council documents themselves. Unfortunately, hierarchical church teaching and practical church structures do not reflect the understanding of these realities as they are proposed in contemporary moral theology. The recent developments in moral theology described above are by no means beyond criticism, but the hierarchical magisterium is often not even in a position to dialogue critically with these developments.

Historical consciousness came to the fore at Vatican II in terms of the recognition for theology to be in dialogue with the modern world, the acceptance of the importance of the signs of the times, and the realization of change and development in church teaching. Historical consciousness as distinguished from classicism gives greater importance to the historical, the particular, and the individual without denying some general universal realities (e.g., the right to life, the dignity of the human person). The best example of the acceptance of historical consciousness in official hierarchical teaching on moral matters is the recognition by Pope Paul VI in *Octogesima adveniens* that in the midst of the widely varying situations in the area of social morality it is not the ambition or the mission of the Petrine office to propose solutions of universal validity. The local Christian communities must arrive at their own solutions in the light of the gospel and of the social teaching of the church.[40] Historical consciousness recognizes the diversity of approaches based on historical and cultural differences. Likewise, the more inductive methodology connected with historical consciousness appreciates the difficulty of arriving at certitude on the level of moral universals in dealing with complex specific questions. Such an understanding grounds the call for greater diversity and even the possibility of dissent in the area of moral norms dealing with complex specific questions.

The United States bishops in their pastoral letters on social matters have called attention to the diversity within the church community on complex questions of justice and peace.[41] However, the bishops have not applied the same recognition of diversity and pluralism to approaches with regard to abortion laws. The hierarchical church teaching office has not recognized that in the matter of so-called private morality one cannot attain a certitude on specific moral norms that will definitely exclude the possibility of error.

Historical consciousness also gives more significance to the role of the subject and the subject's own way of looking at and understanding reality. We need to employ a hermeneutic of suspicion because everyone brings to one's theology one's own prejudices and limitations. There is no such thing as an objective reading of the situation apart from what the subject brings to it. Feminist theology has rightly criticized the unrecognized prejudices present in much theology.

Historical consciousness recognizes a greater pluralism in moral matters, a greater difficulty in achieving absolute certitude, and an appreciation of the limitations affecting the approach of an individual or of any group within society. Yes, there are exaggerations of historical consciousness, but the official church teaching office has not consistently accepted the basic reality itself.

Many moral theologians have an understanding of the nature and role of theology different from that proposed in some contemporary official church documents. A first aspect concerns the pluralism of theologies. Such a pluralism follows from the recognition of historical consciousness. There are many different and acceptable theological approaches within the Catholic faith tradition. No longer can one speak about the perennial theology or the perennial philosophy. However, official church documents do not recognize anything but a Neoscholastic, manualistic theology. By identifying one theology with the faith all other theologies tend to be looked upon as suspect. It is true that some theologies are inadequate, but nevertheless the church must recognize a plurality of possible theologies within the one Catholic faith. In the field of morality, for example, the manualist theologians propose that direct killing or direct abortion is always wrong, but the understanding of direct and indirect is based on one particular philosophical understanding that is not necessarily convincing to many contemporary Catholic moral theologians who would employ a different philosophy. Official church documents seem to use only one theology and reject other approaches as being opposed to the faith. However, there is room for more than only the theology of the Roman school in contemporary Catholicism.

A second aspect of the understanding of theology is more closely connected with ecclesiology. Very often recent church documents understand the role of theology as a continuation of the hierarchical teaching office in the church. As a result, Catholic theologians need a mandate or a mission from the competent ecclesiastical authority. However, most contemporary theologians do not understand their discipline as being merely a continuation of the hierarchical teaching office in the church. The relationship between the two is much more complex. There can be no doubt that the church before the nineteenth century accepted an understanding of theology that was not totally subordinated to explaining and justifying the teaching of the hierarchical magisterium. In fact, theology itself merited the name of magisterium. The complex relationship between theology and the hierarchical magisterium will always be delicate. There should be some tension between the two, but one cannot simplistically reduce the role of theology to that of substantiating the claims of the hierarchical magisterium.[42]

A third important area of differences concerns ecclesiology. A primary question involves the possibility of dissent from authoritative, noninfallible hierarchical teaching in the moral area. In my judgment the whole question of infallibility does not apply to official church teachings on specific moral questions. A more historically conscious methodology recognizes the difficulty of arriving at a certitude that excludes the possibility of error on specific complex moral issues. The complexity involved calls for a greater pluralism and diversity within the church. Contemporary theologians often point to the fact that a proper understanding of the Constitution on the Church (paragraph 25) in its history and context implicitly recognizes the possibility of dissent.[43] However, official hierarchical church documents have had difficulty in explicitly recognizing the possibility of dissent. In a sense the most crucial question today concerns the limits of pluralism and dissent, but the discussion of this significant issue cannot take place until the hierarchical teaching office recognizes the possibility of dissent.

A second ecclesiological concern involves the theoretical and practical recognition that the church is the people of God, a community of equal disciples. Theoretically, Vatican II recognized this reality, but at times the hierarchical aspect of the church is too central and paramount. For example, the Holy Spirit dwells in all the faithful, and through baptism all share in the priestly, ruling, and teaching functions of Jesus. As a result, the teaching function of the total church cannot be absolutely identified with only the hierarchical teaching office. In practice there can be no doubt that the temptation is strong to reduce the church just to the hierarchical offices which should exist in the service of the church.

All agree that Vatican II firmly established the principle of collegiality in the church by emphasizing the role of the bishops. One of the possible dangers of this emphasis is the failure to recognize the role of all the baptized in the church. However, in practice even the principle of collegiality has not really been introduced into the church and church structures in a meaningful way. The recognition of the role of the individual diocesan bishop, of national conferences of bishops, and of the bishops as a whole has not been translated into new structures and made a part of the life of the institutional church. The new Code of Canon Law does not really decentralize the church. Decisions are still made in Rome which are most appropriately made on the local level. Collegiality calls for Catholic ecclesiology to accept the principle of subsidiarity that calls for the more centralized body to intervene only when the more local levels cannot deal properly with the issue.

Instrumentalities such as the Synod of Bishops have really not been a true exercise of collegiality, for they have functioned merely as a consultative body to the pope. Collegiality will not exist in reality until a bishop or group of bishops can say publicly: "Holy Father, we love you. We respect you as the holder of the Petrine office in the church. But in this matter you are wrong."

The church must always live with many tensions, including the tensions between theology and official church teachings. However, at the present time tensions are exaggerated because of the different understandings of historical consciousness, theology, and ecclesiology which are so often dividing theologians from the hierarchical teaching office. The understandings of these three realities generally accepted in contemporary Catholic moral theology are explicitly or implicitly found in Vatican Council II. Unnecessary tensions are going to continue to exist until the hierarchical church is willing to recognize these realities. On the basis of these understandings there can and should be a critical discussion of the substantive proposals made in contemporary moral theology.

This chapter has tried to study the development of Catholic moral theology in the United States in the past twenty years. The analysis has considered the different contexts of moral theology, an overview of its content, and the tensions created in the church by these developments. Twenty years ago I do not think anyone could have predicted what has as a matter of fact occurred. What will happen in the next twenty years?

NOTES

1. Donald E. Pelotte, *John Courtney Murray: Theologian in Conflict* (New York: Paulist Press, 1976).

2. For a recent study by a well-informed journalist on the debate over contraception with heavy emphasis on the papal commission and the American context see Robert Blair Kaiser, *The Politics of Sex and Religion* (Kansas City, MO: Leaven Press, 1985). For a discussion of the contraception debate before 1970 with emphasis on the reactions in the United States see William H. Shannon, *The Lively Debate: Responses to Humanae Vitae* (New York: Sheed and Ward, 1970).

3. Germain G. Grisez, *Contraception and the Natural Law* (Milwaukee: Bruce, 1964).

4. Ibid., p. 20.

5. Ibid., p. 41.

6. John C. Ford and Germain Grisez, "Contraception and Infallibility," *Theological Studies* 39 (1978): 258-312. For a revisionist position see Joseph A. Komonchak, "*Humanae Vitae* and Its Reception: Ecclesiological Reflections," *Theological Studies* 39 (1978): 221-257.

7. Rosemary Rodgers, *A History of the College Theology Society* (Villanova, PA: College Theology Society, 1983). *Horizons* is the journal of the College Theology Society.

8. Anthony Kosnik *et al.*, *Human Sexuality: New Dimensions in American Catholic Thought* (New York: Paulist Press, 1977). For what can accurately be called a conservative response to the above see Ronald Lawler, Joseph Boyle, Jr., and William E. May, *Catholic Sexual Ethics: A Summary, Explanation, and Defense* (Huntington, IN: Our Sunday Visitor, 1985).

9. Raymond E. Brown, "Bishops and Theologians: 'Dispute' Surrounded by Fiction," *Origins* 7 (1978): 673-682.

10. Richard A. McCormick has developed this theory in greater depth than any other ethicist. For the development of his thought see Richard A. McCormick, *Notes on Moral Theology 1965 through 1980* (Washington, DC: University Press of America, 1981); *Notes on Moral Theology 1981 through 1984* (Washington, DC: University Press of America, 1984).

11. President's Commission for the Study of Ethical and Legal Problems in Medicine and Biomedical and Behavioral Research, *Summing Up: Final Report on Studies of the Ethical and Legal Problems in Medicine and Biomedical and Behavioral Research* (Washington, DC: U.S. Government Printing Office, 1983).

12. For many different viewpoints on this question see Charles E. Curran and Richard A. McCormick, eds., *Readings in Moral Theology No. 2: The Distinctiveness of Christian Ethics* (New York: Paulist Press, 1980). Other volumes edited by Curran and McCormick in this series are: *Readings in Moral Theology No. 1: Moral Norms and Catholic Tradition; Readings in Moral Theology No. 3: The Magisterium and Morality; Readings in Moral Theology No. 4: The Use of Scripture in Moral Theology* (New York: Paulist Press, 1979, 1982, 1984).

13. "The Pastoral Letter on War and Peace: The Challenge of Peace: God's Promise and Our Response," *Origins* 13 (1983): 3, 4.

14. Thomas A. Shannon, ed., *War or Peace? The Search for New Answers* (Maryknoll, NY: Orbis Books, 1980). This volume is in a sense a festschrift for Gordon C. Zahn, who has written most extensively on Christian pacifism from the Catholic perspective.

15. David Hollenbach, *Claims in Conflict: Retrieving and Renewing the Catholic Human Rights Tradition* (New York: Paulist Press, 1979); Alfred Hennelly and John Langan, eds., *Human Rights in the Americas: The Struggle for Consensus* (Washington, DC: Georgetown University Press, 1982); Margaret E. Crahan, ed., *Human Rights and Basic Needs in the Americas* (Washington, DC: Georgetown University Press, 1982). All three volumes were written in connection with the Woodstock Theological Center in Washington.

16. Margaret A. Farley, "Feminist Ethics in the Christian Ethics

Curriculum," *Horizons* 11 (1984): 361-372; June O'Connor, "How to Mainstream Feminist Studies by Raising Questions: The Case of the Introductory Course," *Horizons* 11 (1984): 373-392.

17. Edward LeRoy Long, Jr., *Academic Bonding and Social Concern: The Society of Christian Ethics 1959-1983* (no place given: Religious Ethics, 1984).

18. James M. Gustafson, *Protestant and Roman Catholic Ethics: Prospects for Rapprochement* (Chicago: University of Chicago Press, 1978).

19. "Presentation of the Linacre Quarterly Award to Dr. Paul Ramsey by John P. Mullooly, M.D.," *The Linacre Quarterly* 46 (1979): 7, 8.

20. Gustafson, *Protestant and Roman Catholic Ethics*, p. 151. For a fuller development of my analysis see Curran, *Politics, Medicine, and Christian Ethics: A Dialogue with Paul Ramsey* (Philadelphia: Fortress Press, 1973).

21. James M. Gustafson, *Ethics from a Theocentric Perspective*, vol. 1: *Theology and Ethics*; vol. 2: *Ethics and Theology* (Chicago: University of Chicago Press, 1981, 1984).

22. "A Call to Concern," *Christianity and Crisis* 37 (1977): 222-224.

23. Long, *Academic Bonding and Social Concern*, p. 136.

24. Richard Hofstadter and Walter P. Metzger, *Academic Freedom in the United States* (New York: Columbia University Press, 1955).

25. Neil G. McCluskey, ed., *The Catholic University: A Modern Appraisal* (Notre Dame, IN: University of Notre Dame Press, 1970).

26. "Land O'Lakes Statement," in McCluskey, *The Catholic University*, pp. 336ff.

27. Frederick Walter Gunti, "Academic Freedom as an Operative Principle for the Catholic Theologian" (S.T.D. dissertation, The Catholic University of America, 1969).

28. Aldo J. Tos, "A Critical Study of American Views on Academic Freedom" (Ph.D. dissertation, The Catholic University of America, 1958).

29. James John Annarelli, "Academic Freedom and the American Roman Catholic University" (Ph.D. dissertation, Drew University, 1984).

30. Archbishop Rembert G. Weakland, O.S.B., "A Catholic University: Some Clarifications," *Catholic Herald* (March 21, 1985):3.

31. Lay Commission on Catholic Social Teaching and the U.S. Economy, *Toward the Future: Catholic Social Thought and the U.S. Economy: A Lay Letter* (North Tarrytown, NY: Lay Commission, 1984).

32. For Novak's latest work on the subject see Michael Novak,

Freedom with Justice: Catholic Social Thought and Liberal Institutions (San Francisco: Harper and Row, 1984).

33. J. Brian Benestad, *The Pursuit of a Just Social Order: Policy Statements of the U.S. Catholic Bishops, 1966-1980* (Washington, DC: Ethics and Public Policy Center, 1982).

34. Joseph Cardinal Bernardin, "Fordham University Address on the Need for a Consistent Ethic of Life," *Origins* 13 (1984): 491-494; "Enlarging the Dialogue on a Consistent Ethic of Life," *Origins* 13 (1984): 705-709.

35. For the most systematic treatment of his position see Stanley Hauerwas, *The Peaceable Kingdom* (Notre Dame, IN: University of Notre Dame Press, 1983).

36. Timothy E. O'Connell, *Principles for a Catholic Morality* (New York: Seabury Press, 1978).

37. Daniel C. Maguire, *The Moral Choice* (Garden City, NY: Doubleday, 1978).

38. Bernard Häring, *Free and Faithful in Christ: Moral Theology for Clergy and Laity*, 3 vols. (New York: Seabury Press, 1978, 1979, 1981).

39. Germain Grisez, *The Way of the Lord Jesus*, vol. 1: *Christian Moral Principles* (Chicago: Franciscan Herald Press, 1983).

40. Pope Paul VI, *Octogesima adveniens*, par. 4, in David J. O'Brien and Thomas A. Shannon, eds., *Renewing the Earth: Catholic Documents on Peace, Justice and Liberation* (Garden City, NY: Doubleday Image Books, 1977), pp. 353, 354.

41. "The Pastoral Letter on War and Peace," *Origins* 13 (1983): 2, 3.

42. James A. Coriden, "Book III: The Teaching Office in the Church," in James A. Coriden, Thomas J. Green, and Donald E. Heintschl, eds., *The Code of Canon Law: A Text and Commentary* (New York: Paulist Press, 1985), pp. 543-589.

43. Joseph A. Komonchak, "Ordinary Papal Magisterium and Religious Assent," in Charles E. Curran, ed., *Contraception: Authority and Dissent* (New York: Herder and Herder, 1969), pp. 101-126.

3: What Is Distinctive and Unique about Christian Ethics and Christian Morality?

In the United States the question has recently been proposed, "What is specific and distinctive in Christian ethics and Christian morality?" The most significant, or at least the second most significant, debate in Catholic moral theology in Germany in the 1970s involved the dispute between the proponents of an autonomous morality and those who proposed an ethic of faith. This chapter will touch on three aspects involved in these current discussions — theological ethics as ethics, the material content of Christian morality, and the role and function of Christian ethics.

I. Theological Ethics as Ethics

Theological ethics is a species of ethics and hence pursues the same basic questions as any ethics and has the same formal structure. All ethics tries to respond to the same questions concerning what is the good, what are the values and goals to pursue, what attitudes and dispositions should characterize the person, what acts are right or wrong. One speaks today of different ethical models — the teleological, which seeks the good; the deontological, which is concerned with the right; and the responsibility model, which pursues the fitting. These three approaches or models can adequately describe various possible approaches to Christian ethics or to any other type of ethics.

Is there anything so distinctive and characteristic of Christian ethics that Christian ethics by definition would fit into one of these models rather than another? Any understanding of the history of Christian ethics shows that there has been and continues to be a diversity of models used. Divine-command theories are a form of the deontological model, whereas Thomas Aquinas employed a teleological model, beginning with the question of the ultimate end of human beings. In contemporary Christian ethics all these approaches have been proposed and used. The basic concept of Christian love has been understood and interpreted in accord with these three different approaches. Christian love has been described in teleological terms as the goal to be achieved or even as the greatest good of the greatest number. Deontologists see Christian love as the norm or the right thing to do. For others Christian love is the fitting thing. Individual Christian ethicists will properly argue for one position rather than another, but there is no inherent basis in Christian ethics itself why one of the possible ethical models should be chosen or why another should be eliminated.

Thus theological ethics is a species of ethics which has the same formal structure and raises and tries to respond to the same questions as all other ethics. Most contemporary Christian ethicists seem to agree with this understanding, although some in the Barthian tradition understand Christian ethics as distinct from any other type of ethics.

II. The Material Content of Christian Morality

The obvious difference between theological ethics and philosophical ethics comes from the sources of ethical wisdom and knowledge. Philosophical ethics is restricted to human reason and the whole realm of the human. Theological ethics, and in our particular case, Christian ethics, also recognizes the theological sources of faith, revelation, and grace. Within Christian ethics there has been and continues to be a debate about the exact role of reason. Many would give some role to reason as a source of ethical wisdom and knowlege.

This present section will narrow the discussion to the material content of Christian morality and its relationship to the material content of other morality. In this discussion I am understanding Christian ethics as a thematic, systematic, and methodological approach to the understanding of Christian morality. The material content of Christian morality refers to the norms, decisions, virtues, goals, values, and dispositions which are normative for Christian persons and actions in the world.

Recent developments in Roman Catholic moral theology have influenced the approaches taken to this question of the relationship of the material content of Christian morality to human morality. The manuals of Catholic moral theology in the pre-Vatican II period based their approach to the rightness and wrongness of moral action on the natural law. Such a moral theology with its specific aim of training confessors as judges for the sacrament of penance was rightly criticized for being extrinsic, minimalistic, and legalistic. In the 1960s renewal in Catholic moral theology involved giving greater importance to the scriptures and to the role of faith and grace.[1] Vatican II recognized the need for this by insisting that the scriptures were the soul of all theology, and all theology had to be renewed in the light of the scriptures.[2] Such an emphasis was obviously influenced by dialogue with Protestant ethics. A purely natural law ethic was too minimalistic and did not recognize the supernatural aspect of Christian existence. The scripture, faith, grace, and revelation add the supernatural aspect to the material content of the purely natural law morality based on reason and human nature.

However, in subsequent years new problems and debates arose. In the middle 1960s the issue of greatest significance in Catholic moral theology was that of the use of artificial contraception in marriage. The questioning of the Catholic teaching on artificial contraception brought with it a question of moral theory and of the role of the teaching authority of the church in the matter of morals. This debate and the larger issues involved in it became a point of division among Roman

Catholic ethicists. Those opposing the official teaching maintained that such a teaching throughout its history claimed to be based on the natural law and reason. Since the teaching was not convincing to human reason, then it was wrong, and the teaching authority of the church was in error. Many proponets of the official teaching maintained that reason is always subject to human weakness and distortion, but in faith we believe that the Holy Spirit guides the church through the teaching office of the pope and bishops. Thus the discussion over artificial contraception entailed a dispute about the roles of reason and faith in moral theology.[3]

It was precisely the contraception issue which set the stage for a debate among Catholic moral theologians in Germany about autonomous morality. Alfons Auer of Tübingen proposed his theory of autonomous morality, which refers to the fact that concrete norms proposed for Christian living in the world are based on human reason and are communicable to all other human beings. Yes, the Christian relationship to God is all important and constitutes a new horizon of meaning, but this relationship is on the transcendental level, not the categorical level. This Christian horizon of meaning gives a new and profound meaning to our moral life and actions, influences our intentionality, and acts as a stimulator and a critic, but the concrete material norms are not changed by it. Such norms are autonomous and not dependent on faith; thus they are able to be communicated to all human beings. Auer and other proponents of an autonomous morality mention that such a position is in continuity with Thomas Aquinas and the Roman Catholic tradition in general.[4] The opposition to Auer's position became known as an ethic of faith and has been identified especially with B. Stöckle and K. Hilpert.[5] H.U. von Balthasar and J. Ratzinger also appear to favor this position, but their writings in the area have not been that numerous.[6] Stöckle objects to the concept of autonomy and to the optimism of Auer's approach. Faith and the scriptures must also affect the material content of Christian ethics. It is significant that the majority of the German moral theologians have accepted with some modifications the position proposed by Auer. The theologians supporting an autonomous morality generally can be described as progressive, and they dissent from official church teachings on certain questions that have been under discussion in the literature. The proponents of an ethic of faith are described as more conservative and generally suport the official teaching of the church on moral matters, for such an official teaching office is part of what faith gives to the Catholic.

On looking back one may see two different tendencies in the "progressive" position of Catholic moral theology in the past two decades. In the decade of the 1960s great emphasis was given to the need for renewal based on revelation, grace, and faith as distinguished from reason and the natural. The material content of Christian morality was distinguished from the material content of human or rational morality. However, in the 1970s we can perceive a shift in the sense that the more "progressive" moral theologians of this decade were arguing very strongly that the material content of normative Christian morality must be communicable to all human beings, and faith itself does not add anything to it.

My own attempt to deal with the questions raised ultimately finds its theological basis in anthropology. The older understanding of nature and grace sees grace as something gratuitously added to the order of nature. Supernature is added on top of nature, and consequently the material moral content of the supernatural order adds something to the natural order. However, many contemporary Catholic theologians, especially Karl Rahner, have proposed a different anthropology which does not involve a two-layer understanding of human beings. Pure nature as such never existed. God calls all historically existing human beings to share in the fullness of God's love and self-communication. Even those who claim to be atheists may on the transcendental level be truly responding to God's self-communication in love. The only human beings we know are called to share in the fullness of God's self-gift. There is no such thing historically as the purely natural order to which the supernatural is added. God's self-communication offers to all the fullness of what it means to be human.

The explicit Christian gift and response bring Christians to the fullness of humanity. Such an understanding of theological anthropology influences one's whole approach to revelation, grace, Christology, and the other theological disciplines.

In the light of this theological anthropology there is only one history; not a sacred history and a secular history. This recognition has significant consequences for the role of the church and the gospel in our world. Since there is only one history, the church and the community of disciples of Jesus are not a sect who are set against the world. Christians are striving with all people of good will to make the world more just. The recognition of the one historical order lies behind the celebrated phrase of the 1971 Synod of Bishops that action on behalf of justice and the transformation of the world are a constitutive dimension of the preaching of the gospel and of the mission of the church. The requirements of justice which are appropriate in this one existing historical order are something that must be available to all human beings.

Such a theological anthropology has been the basis for my position that the normative material content of Christian morality is in principle open to and knowable by all other human beings. In terms of the material content of morality (whether it be virtues, goals, dispositions, values, or norms), what is proposed for Christian human beings as such and for their life in human society, there is no exclusively Christian content that differs from what is to be required of all others.

To clarify my position it will help to enter into dialogue with others who have written on the subject.[7] In general I share the conclusion proposed by the approach of autonomous morality, but there are some differences. First of all I am basing my approach, not on an abstract metaphysical concept of human nature, but on the historical reality that all human beings today are called to share in the fullness of God's loving self-communication. Defenders of an autonomous morality often give the impression of basing their position on such an abstract metaphysical concept of nature.

Second, autonomous morality admits that the normative content of Christian morality is autonomous in the sense that it can stand on its own apart from the contribution of faith. However, the normative content appears to be reduced to minimal universal norms that are to apply to life in society. I do not want to reduce the normative content of morality only to norms. Dispositions, attitudes, values, and goals are all part of the normative content of Christian morality. However, I am referring to those virtues, values, dispositions, goals, and norms that are proposed for all Christians and not just for particular individuals with particular vocations.

Third, supporters of an autonomous morality see the contribution of the scriptures and of faith in terms of *parenesis* as distinguished from normative ethics.[8] *Parenesis* presupposes that the act is morally right or wrong. The scriptures generally assume that a particular action is good or bad and then give motivation, stimulation, etc. At the very minimum, if one sees moral content as involving more than universal norms or the judgment of whether a particular act is good or bad, then a greater role can be given to the normative moral content found in the scriptures and in faith. Scripture does describe the values, dispositions, and goals that should be a part of human existence. In my judgment faith and the scriptures cannot be reduced only to *parenesis*; they also contribute to normative morality. This position coheres not only with my second point that the material content or normative morality involves more than universal laws and judgments about particular acts but also with my basic anthropological understanding. There is only the one historical humanity and moral order, not both a natural and a supernatural order, and all are capable of knowing it. The Christian tries to understand this order in the light of the Christian story, symbols, and self-understanding. Those who are not Christian can arrive at the same moral content but not use the Christian way of arriving at it. Christian faith and the scriptures do contain normative moral content and not merely exhortation or *parenesis*, but such content is in principle open to all human beings.

Fourth, I think the term autonomous is not felicitous. At the very minimum one must explain that such autonomy is not opposed to theonomy and the divine-human relationship properly understood. Autonomy also has the ring of individualism about it. I prefer the term human or truly human morality.

My position can be further clarified by a continuing discussion with Norbert Rigali, who has frequently written on this subject and has devoted a recent article to analyzing and criticizing my position.[9] Rigali rightly points out some of the developments that appeared in my own thinking over the years, such as my recognizing that the subject matter under discussion should have always been described as the normative content of Christian morality rather than Christian ethics. In addition he also indicates my acceptance of his distinction between essentialist and existentialist ethics. However, I would disagree with his analysis that only much later in my own development did I recognize that Christian morality dealt with more than merely moral norms minimally required for all. In my articles on the question of a specifically Christian morality I have consistently recognized that the content of Christian morality also involves virtues, attitudes, goals, values, and dispositions.[10] In my other writings on Christian ethics I have constantly recognized that Christian ethics includes much more than the questions about norms and the morality of particular acts. However, my greatest disagreement with Rigali focuses on his understanding of where my position should logically move in the future.

Rigali's thesis is that my position has given growing emphasis to historical consciousness and must now logically abandon the concept of an essentialist morality based on natural law. The classicist essence is an abstraction from historical culture and society.

Over ten years ago in discussing my first article on the subject Rigali pointed out that the position I maintain, namely, that others can and do arrive at the same ethical conclusions, dispositions, and attitudes as Christians, was true within the range of essentialist ethics. But in addition to essentialist ethics there also exists an existentialist ethics in terms of the particular individual person and an "essential ethic of Christianity" which refers to the person as a member of the Christian community with different specific moral obligations arising from membership in that community.[11] I later accepted this distinction as being helpful and clarifying what I was trying to say.[12]

However in his latest article Rigali now abandons the former distinction. Only within the confines of an outmoded classicism can one make a distinction between the essential and the existential. He goes on to assert that in the light of historical consciousness the natural law morality of classicism cannot be identified with real morality. Real morality is the historical morality that has been created by various communities in the world. Thus there is a specifically Christian morality and a specifically Christian ethics.

My first reaction is that we might not be speaking about the same thing. I am talking about the normative material content which is posed in Christian morality for all. From the very beginning of the discussion, despite my inaccurate use of the term Christian ethics, my thesis has been that non-Christians can and do arrive at the same ethical conclusions and prize the same proximate dispositions, goals, and attitudes as Christians. As examples, I mentioned such attitudes, goals, and dispositions as self-sacrificing love, freedom, hope, concern for the neighbor in need, and even the realization that one finds one's life in losing it.

I still could use Rigali's concept of essentialist ethics as distinguished from existentialist ethics and from essential Christian ethics to describe my position, but I would not interpret essential in the same way that Rigali now understands it. Rigali understands essentialist ethics as based on an abstract natural law of essence. However, such was never the way I approached the problem. In my very first article on the question in 1970[10] I distinguished my approach from one based on a traditional, abstract natural law approach. My position starts from the *de facto* historically existing anthropology in which all are offered God's saving self-communication and in which there is only one given historical moral order. My basis is primarily theological and not philosophical, beginning with the only existing concrete historical order. I accepted Rigali's use of the word essential to describe the moral order whose normative content is the same for all as distinguished from the existential call of an individual and the obligations arising from membership in the Christian church as such. My position can be described as "in-principled." In principle all other human beings can arrive at the same moral norms governing human action and the same values, virtues, dispositions, and goals that should characterize our moral selves. This in-principled statement does not in any way claim that all people do arrive at the same material content. Obviously many people do not. Historicity affects all, but both Christians and non-Christians are called to share the love and life of the one God.

One further point must be mentioned. There is a great danger of interpreting my theological anthropology in an overly optimistic manner. I have criticized the Pastoral Constitution on the Church in the Modern World of the Second Vatican Council precisely because of its overly optimistic anthropology. To avoid this danger I have insisted on the continuing presence of sin in the world and the fact that the fullness of the eschaton will never come in this world.

III. The Role and Function of Christian Ethics

If one recognizes that in principle the normative moral content that Christianity proposes is not exclusively Christian but that in principle all can arrive at this content, the question arises what is the role and function of Christian ethics.

Christian ethics as a reflexive, systematic science studies the moral life from the distinctively Christian perspective. Such an ethics relies on the sources of ethical wisdom and knowledge proper to Christian self-understanding. Faith, revelation, grace, sin, scriptures, and tradition, as well as the teachings of the church, all enter into the picture. Also my understanding gives an important role to human reason. (In the light of the limited scope of this essay it is impossible to go further into the relationship of all these sources to each other.) Christian ethics as scientific reflection on the Christian moral life must use all these sources.

Recall that the reality of Christian morality includes more

than the normative material content. Christian morality includes Christian intentionalities and motivations. Although
I have argued that the normative material content of Christian morality is in principle available to all other human beings, it does not follow that Christian moral experience or
Christian ethics arrives at these values, virtues, goals dispositions, norms, and particular judgments by prescinding from
the distinctively Christian sources of ethical wisdom and
knowledge. The proper function of Christian ethics is to address all questions concerning morality, including normative
moral content, in the light of the Christian self-understanding
and of all the distinctively Christian sources. From this perspective I reject the position of Timothy O'Connell that Christian ethics is philosophical ethics.[13]

In addition to this normal role and function of Christian
ethics there can also be a secondary and supplemental function of approaching a content question by prescinding from
the specifically Christian self-understanding. Such an approach
has been proposed by Enda McDonagh in his Christian theology of morality.[14] The primary purpose of such an approach,
in my judgment, is to communicate the moral teaching to
others who do not share the same Christian self-understanding.
The pastoral letter of the American Catholic bishops on peace
and war well illustrates this understanding.[15] The letter
recognizes that there is only one moral order which is the same
for all. It addresses the members of the church in the light
of a specifically Christian self-understanding, but it also attempts to communicate with all people of good will and thus
at times prescinds from the specifically Christian.

In addition other reasons exist for this secondary and supplemental function of Christian ethics. One is an apologetic
function in showing that Christian moral content corresponds
to the best of human moral aspirations and knowledge. At
the same time such an approach also can serve as a critique
and dialogue partner with the proper role of Christian ethics.

In summary, Christian ethics primarily and properly appeals to the distinctively Christian sources in reflecting scientifically on the Christian moral life. However, the normative moral content proposed for all Christians apart from the specific obligations referring to their membership in the church is morally communicable to all human beings. There is a limited but important secondary function in Christian ethics in trying to show that this moral content is *per se* open to and required of all.

NOTES

1. The most influential work in the renewal of moral theology was Bernard Häring, *The Law of Christ*, 3 vols. (Westminster, MD: Newman Press, 1961-1966).

2. Dogmatic Constitution on Divine Revelation, n. 24, and Decree on Priestly Formation, n. 16, in Walter M. Abbott, ed., *The Documents of Vatican II* (New York: Guild Press, 1966), pp. 127, 452.

3. Joseph A. Selling, "The Reaction to *Humanae Vitae*: A Study in Special and Fundamental Theology" (S.T.D. dissertation, Catholic University of Louvain, 1977).

4. Alfons Auer, "Nach dem Erscheinen der Enzyklika *Humanae Vitae*: Zen These über die Findung sittlicher Weisungen," *Theologisches Quartalschrift* 149 (1969): 75-85; Auer, *Autonome Moral und christlicher Glaube* (Dusseldorf: Patmos, 1971).

5. B. Stöckle, *Grenzen der autonomen Moral* (München: Kosel, 1974); Stockle, *Handeln aus dem Glauben: Moraltheologie konkret* (Freiburg: Herder, 1977); K. Hilpert, *Ethik und Rationalität: Untersuchungen zum Autonomieproblem und zu seiner Bedeutung für die theologische Ethik* (Dusseldorf: Patmos, 1980).

6. H. U. von Balthasar, "Neun Satze zur christlichen Ethik," in *Prinzipien christlicher Moral*, ed. J. Ratzinger (Einsiedeln: Johannes Verlag, 1976); J. Ratzinger, "Lehramt-Glaube-Moral," in *Prinzipien christlichen Moral*, pp, 43-66.

7. For various positions on all sides of the broader debate about the distinctiveness and uniqueness of Christian ethics see Charles E. Curran and Richard A. McCormick, eds., *Readings in Moral Theology No. 2: The Distinctiveness of Christian Ethics* (New York: Paulist Press, 1980).

8. Werner Wolbert, "Parensi ed etica normativa," *Rivista di Teologia Morale* 49 (1981): 11-39.

9. Norbert J. Rigali, "Charles Curran's Understanding of Christian Ethics," *Chicago Studies* 22 (1983): 123-132.

10. Charles E. Curran, "Is There a Distinctively Christian Social Ethic?" in Philip D. Morris, ed., *Metropolis: Christian Presence and Responsibility* (Notre Dame, IN: Fides, 1970), pp. 92-120, especially pp. 114, 115; reprinted in Curran, *Catholic Moral Theology in Dialogue* (Notre Dame, IN: University of Notre Dame Press, 1976), pp. 1-23.

11. Norbert J. Rigali, "On Christian Ethics," *Chicago Studies* 10 (1971): 227-247.

12. Charles E. Curran, "Is There a Catholic and/or Christian Ethic?" in *Proceedings of the Catholic Theological Society of America* 29 (1974): 124-154; also found in Curran, *Ongoing Revision: Studies in Moral Theology* (Notre Dame, IN: Fides, 1975), pp. 1-36.

13. Timothy E. O'Connell, *Principles for a Catholic Morality* (New York: Seabury Press, 1978), pp. 40-41; 199-208.

14. Enda McDonagh, *Gift and Call: Towards a Christian Theology of Morality* (St. Meinrad, IN: Abbey Press, 1975); see also his later collection of essays, *Doing the Truth: The Quest for Moral Theology* (Notre Dame, IN: University of Notre Dame Press 1979).

15. Pastoral Letter of the American Catholic Bishops "The Challenge of Peace: God's Promise and Our Response," *Origins* 13 (May 19, 1983): 1-32.

4: Moral Theology in Dialogue with Biomedicine and Bioethics

The progress made in medicine and genetics in the last few decades has been outstanding. Developments in preventive medicine have been occurring since the beginning of the century as is illustrated in the tremendous advance in the life expectancy of people first in the more industrialized countries but now in all parts of the globe. However, the dramatic changes in therapeutic medicine have received most of the attention in the last few decades. Heart transplant operations have made the headlines of newspapers throughout the world ever since the first attempt by Dr. Barnard in 1967. *In vitro* fertilization with embryo transfer has made it possible for infertile couples to have children, but this amazing technological breakthrough has raised moral questions about the meaning of human parenthood, the use of surrogate mothers, and the status of the embryo.[1] Startling experiments in genetics have made genetic surgery, genetic engineering, and eugenics important topics of discussion.

These medical and genetic breakthroughs have also affected the daily lives of people. Medical technology can prolong life at its end. Respiration and circulation can be extended for an indefinite time. Probably every family existing today in the United States has already or shortly will deal with the question of whether or not to cease treatment for a dying family member. The developing technology has also occasioned the need to rethink the criterion or test for death precisely because circulation and respiration can be continued artificially.

These dramatic and comparatively recent developments have had important ramifications in the area of biomedical

65

ethics. Before 1960 medical ethics in the United States and elsewhere in the world was confined mostly to Roman Catholic moral theology.[2] Other early Christian authors in the field included Joseph Fletcher in the United States and Helmut Thielicke in West Germany.[3] In the last twenty-five years an entirely new discipline of bioethics has emerged. Theological ethicists were early leaders in the discipline, but now people from many other disciplines have interested themselves in bioethics. The literature spawned by this new discipline is enormous. Articles, books, and bibliographies on bioethics abound. Many journals have come into existence in the last few years dealing only with these types of questions. The *Encyclopedia of Bioethics* was published in 1978.[4] In addition to the growth of bioethics courses in medical schools and other academic institutions, think tanks dealing with bioethics have sprung up throughout the United States and Canada.

The public importance of bioethics has been underlined in the United States by the boards and committees put together under government auspices to address these problems. The latest and perhaps the best known of these was The President's Commission for the Study of Ethical Problems in Medicine and Biomedical and Behavioral Research. This committee of eleven started its work in January 1980 with a definite time limit which was ultimately extended to March 31, 1983. The commission, whose function was advisory and not regulatory, produced ten reports, five appendix volumes, and a guidebook for institutional review boards. The reports dealt with decisions to forego life-sustaining treatment, the definition of death, informed consent, experimentation, access to health care, genetic manipulation, and other issues.[5] Many people today are calling for a permanent commission to continue the monitoring of biomedical developments and technologies.[6] Thus, in the last twenty-five years the significant concerns raised by biomedical advances has occasioned an entirely new discipline to emerge and prosper.

What are the effects of these developments on Catholic moral theology? This essay will concentrate on four important areas: historical consciousness, anthropology, eschatology and theological concerns, and the nature and growth of moral theology in the light of its relationship to contemporary bioethics.

I. Historical Consciousness

The first significant effect of these developments in biomedical science and technology and in the growth of the discipline of bioethics confirms the importance of a historically conscious worldview. Chapter one contrasted historical consciousness with a classicist approach that stresses the eternal, the immutable, and the unchanging. Historical consciousness gives more importance to the particular, the individual, and the changing. A classicist approach tends toward a deductive methodology, whereas historical consciousness gives more emphasis to an inductive methodology. A classicist understanding of natural law sees the natural law as a somewhat detailed plan of God for the world, to which the individual and the community must conform. Historical consciousness recognizes that the human is developing and changing, and human beings have the responsibility to make and keep human life more human.

The scientific and technological developments in biomedicine emphasize that humankind is not something static, given once and for all, but is rather changing and developing. This change is something not totally built into human nature and programmed in advance, but rather is the achievement of human creativity and initiative. Biomedical breakthroughs testify to the creativity and initiative of human beings who have a responsibility to bring about a more humane existence.

A classicist worldview would be most reluctant to admit that the discipline of moral theology itself could or should change. The science of moral theology always remains the same, with only different applications to the new problems and questions that emerge. Historical consciousness understands the discipline of moral theology somewhat differently. History itself shows that moral theology has changed and developed throughout the course of the centuries.[7] The moral theology of the manuals from the time of the Council of Trent until Vatican II was highly colored by the pastoral purpose of training priests to exercise their function as confessors with special emphasis on their role as judges. Moral theology exists in history and therefore is very much affected by the circumstances in which it finds itself. Moral theology by its very nature reflects on the lived experience of the Christian community, which is revealed in the Scriptures, witnessed to in the tradition, celebrated in the liturgy, and practiced in contemporary life. Moral theology as systematic and thematic reflection on this understanding of the Christian life will definitely be colored by contemporary experience and self-understanding without, however, in any way absolutizing the contemporary and the present. A historically conscious worldview recognizes that the discipline of moral theology itself does not remain static, so that it is appropriate and necessary to look at the changes in the discipline brought about by modern biomedicine and the emerging discipline of bioethics.

Historical consciousness, however, recognizes both continuity and discontinuity and is opposed to the static worldview of classicism as well as to sheer existentialism. Such an existentialism so emphasizes the now that it neglects important connections of the present to the past and the future and also forgets the significant relationships binding the person here and now to other persons and communities. Medical and genetic advances raise new questions, but they also raise with a greater intensity questions which have previously been discussed in the literature of moral theology. In the light of contemporary medicine most families in the industrial world will face the problem of terminating life-supporting technologies. To its credit, Catholic moral theology has a history of sustained discussion of this problem with its traditional distinction between ordinary and extraordinary means.[8] Without denying the value of the principle behind this distinction, even the 1980 Declaration on Euthanasia of the Sacred Congregation for the Doctrine of the Faith maintains that the older terminology is not adequate and suggests the new phrasing of proportionate and disproportionate means.[9] This entire discussion about the means of prolonging life well illustrates historical consciousness at work.

Genetic discoveries may make available many new possibilities, but even some of the most spectacular possibilities are governed by basic moral principles developed in the past. Genetic surgery in the future may be able to treat and change a defective gene but such a procedure (provided it does not deal with reproductive cells) is still governed by the principle of totality. This principle of totality maintains that the harm done to a part of the body must be proportionate to the good of the whole person. History, however, reminds us of the developments that occurred in Catholic moral theology when the question of transplants *inter vivos* first arose. Since the transplant procedure involves harm to one person in order to help another person, most Catholic theologians maintained that such transplants could not be justified on the basis of the principle of totality. Some Catholic theologians therefore concluded that transplants were always wrong. However, other theologians invoked the concept of charity to justify transplants when there is a due proportion. Catholic theology has subsequently agreed on the acceptance of transplants in principle.[10]

Thus a developing historical consciousness plays an important twofold role in the consideration of moral theology and biomedicine. As moral theology looks at biomedical advances, it must recognize that newer discoveries and technologies will and should occur, but not every change or possibility is necessarily for the good. Historical consciousness with its recognition of both continuity and discontinuity must be critical and not merely baptize every technological breakthrough. At the same time historical consciousness demands that the discipline of moral theology recognizes how this dialogue might affect and change moral theology's own self-understanding. The subsequent points treated in this study will illustrate this twofold function of historical consciousness at work.

II. Anthropology

Biomedical advances have brought into sharp focus the whole question of anthropology. Human beings have more power than ever before over their lives. People are able to plan their families. Scientific breakthroughs have given human beings the opportunity to triumph over many different types of disease from polio to malaria. Hopefully science can soon even find a cure for cancer. Some futurists talk about the eugenic possibilities of creating better and more perfect human beings, as biomedical science and technology have given human beings this greater power and control over their lives.

Almost from the very beginning of these discussions about genetics the question has been raised about human beings trying to usurp and play the role of God.[11] It is interesting that accusations of human beings usurping the role of God have often come from outside the tradition of Catholic moral theology. There are obvious limits concerning finite, created human beings which all theological traditions generally admit. However, in the Catholic theological tradition the relationship between God and human beings has never been seen in terms of opposition or rivalry, as if by giving more power to human beings one takes away power from God. Catholic theology rightly stresses the concepts of participation and mediation. We human beings share and participate in the glory, the power, and the goodness of God. The Catholic tradition has made its own the patristic saying that the glory of God is the human being come alive. Human life, human wisdom, human beauty, and human power are reflections of and participations in the life, wisdom, beauty, and power of God. Thomas Aquinas begins his consideration of what today would be called moral theology with the recognition that the human being is an image of God precisely insofar as one is endowed with intellect, free will, and the power of self-determination.[12] By our free, rational self-determination we are images of God and participate in God's self-determination. Self-determination is not usurping God's role but rather is the glory of the human person and of God.

The greater power that human beings achieve by scientific understanding and technological capabilities is not necessarily usurping the role of God. Yes, human beings are limited and finite, but they are called to use their God-given powers of intellect and will to guide and direct their own lives. Biomedical advances above all point up the ability of human beings to interfere with and change the biological and physical orders. Dialogue with biomedicine has been one of the factors influencing many contemporary Catholic moral theologians to a revised understanding of anthropology. Revisionist moral theologians maintain that the anthropology of the manuals of moral theology is guilty of physicalism. Physicalism too readily identifies the physical or biological aspect with the moral or the human aspect of the act.

The biological or the physical is just one aspect of the total human and is not necessarily always identified with the moral and the human. For truly human purposes one can at times interfere with the physical and biological aspects of human existence. In most areas Catholic moral theology has not identified the physical or the biological with the moral, but in medical ethics this has been done with greater frequency. Thus, for example, the tradition has rightly distinguished between the physical act of killing and the moral act of murder, between the physical act of taking something from another and the moral act of stealing. However, often in the area of medical ethics the physical has been equated with the moral and the human. Artificial insemination with a husband's seed has been declared wrong because human reproduction requires the presence of the physical procreative act whereby the semen of the husband is deposited in the vagina of the female. The physical act must always be present and cannot be interfered with or substituted for. The possibility of artificial insemination has made many moral theologians question the older position as being based on a false identification of the physical and the human.[13] For the same reason many Catholic moral theologians disagree with the older condemnation of artificial contraception, direct sterilization, and the concept of directly done evil which is defined on the basis of the physical causality of the act itself.

There can be no doubt that the discussion about physicalism lies at the heart of the differences existing between the two approaches to Catholic medical ethics today. This same problem lies at the root of the contemporary discussion about norms in Catholic moral theology.[14] While revisionist theologians claim that the older anthropology suffers from physicalism, defenders of the older approach claim that the revisionists are gnostic and dualistic because they do not pay enough attention to the body.[15] A full discussion of this important topic cannot be done within the parameters of this present essay. It is sufficient for the purposes of this article to show that developments in biomedical science and technology have been an important influence on the anthropology of many contemporary Catholic moral theologians.

Biomedical technologies point up the ability of human beings to intervene in the biological order, and thus they emphasize the greater freedom and control that human beings have over their lives. Karl Rahner sees these developments as evidence of the ability of human beings to be self-creators.[16] The human person holds one's fate and destiny in one's own hands and is called to create one's own moral self. However, a proper anthropology must not only recognize the power and freedom of human beings in and through biomedical technologies but also the limitations of the human and especially of technology.

The human person cannot be understood totally as a freedom event, for human existence by its very nature is embodied existence. While opposed to a physicalism that absolutizes the physical or biological aspects of the human, I do not want to deny the importance of the physical. At times the physical and the moral or human are the same. The best illustration of this is our own existence. Human existence as we know it in this world is a bodily existence. Without our physical bodily existence we do not exist as human persons. The different tests proposed for determining human death (e.g., cessation of respiration, circulation, or brain function) are based on physical, bodily functioning.

Recent developments have called for new tests to determine if death has occurred.[17] In the past the generally accepted sign of death was the lack of breathing. Breath itself in many languages is intimately connected with spirit or life. Heartbeat was another test for the presence of life. However, recent developments have called attention to the insufficiency of the presence of breathing or of a heartbeat as signs of life. Today respiration and circulation can be kept going artificially.

For this reason there is general agreement that brain death is a more accurate test for death. There are debates about how exactly brain death is determined, but there is general agreement that the insufficiency of the older tests calls for a new test to be used at least in some cases. However, the new test itself (i.e., brain death) like the older tests is based on a physical reality. Thus one must always give great importance to the biological and the physical and recognize that at times the human and the physical are identical.

The human person is limited in and through one's bodily existence. We are limited by our corporeality to being in only one place at one time. We experience fatigue and bodily pain. Human existence cannot be reduced only to freedom. Human beings are limited by the very fact of their humanity and their bodiliness. There is a danger that a one-sided view of the human person as a freedom event will forget about the existence of human limitations. We are not free to intervene any way we want in our humanity. We cannot and/or should not change some things about our own humanity. In an analogous manner the recent emphasis on environmental ethics has reminded us of the human arrogance that forgets to accept physical limitation. Human beings live together with a very complex ecosystem and are not free to arbitrarily intervene and do whatever they want. Humans must respect the environment with which they live. So too in medicine and genetics there are important limitations on what human beings can and should do. Yes, it is very important to recognize that developments in biomedicine have given human beings much more freedom and much more power over their lives, but nonetheless significant limitations will be present. It would be wrong to so extol human freedom and possibilities that one forgets inherent human limitations.

The physical and the biological aspects of human existence are very important and must be given due importance in any adequate anthropology. However, the biological and the physical cannot be absolutized. The traditional Catholic position maintaining that there is no obligation to use extraordinary means to preserve human life and existence recognizes that physical human existence is not an absolute for the believer.

Pope Pius XII in 1957 pointed out that "life, death, all temporal activities are in fact subordinated to spiritual ends."[18] Thus the questions raised by biomedicine and genetics point to the need for proper anthropology that recognizes a greater power of human beings over their lives than in the past, points out the danger of always identifying the physical with the human, and yet recognizes the limitations brought upon human beings by bodily existence.

III. Eschatology and Theological Anthropology

Biomedical advances have not only been in dialogue with our understanding of historical consciousness and of anthropology, but also there has been a relationship between these advances and what might be termed eschatology and theological anthropology. These new developments relate very much to our understanding of eschatology and theological anthropology, and in turn the approach taken to these developments is influenced by eschatology and theological anthropology. Under this general heading of eschatology the following aspects will be treated: human progress and scientific progress; the understanding of biomedicine with its technological developments as a limited good which can, however, be abused; the tragic aspect of human existence; and the basis of human dignity.

No one can deny the startling progress made in biomedicine. This growth has made contemporary theorists more aware of the historical dimension of human existence. From a theological perspective the question is often posed in terms of eschatology. How does this progress in biomedicine relate to the reign of God? How do eschatology and theology view human progress in general and more specifically biomedical progress? What effects have the recent developments had on our view of eschatology? That medicine and genetics have made great strides cannot be denied. However, there has also been a growing concern about the issues and problems raised by biomedical progress. Such a general outlook corresponds with a theological understanding which recognizes that the reign of God through Jesus and the Spirit is already present in our world, but the fullness of the reign of God will come only at the end of time.

Such an eschatology rejects the view that life is only a valley of tears and a time of waiting for the reign of God to truly begin at the end of time. Especially in social ethics in the last century this pie-in-the-sky eschatology has been severely criticized. However, at the same time contemporary experience and theological reflection should reject a progressively developing and steadily evolutionary progress capable of achievement in this world. My theological stance recognizes the basic but limited and finite goodness of creation, the presence and influence of sin which pervades all but does not destroy the basic goodness of all that God has made, the presence of redemptive love as symbolized by faith in the incarnation and redemption, and the recognition that the fullness of the reign of God will come only at the end of time. Such a vision recognizes some possibility of human progress in this world but emphasizes that the fullness will only come at the end of time and that human progress in this world will always be colored by accompanying human finitude and sin. Discussion about the possibilities and problems created by biomedicine support such an eschatological view. Not every change or development is necessarily truly human progress. Eschatology gives us an impetus to work for human progress but at the same time makes one critical of possible dangers. While open to some truly human progress in this world, this eschatological vision refuses to baptize all possible developments as progress.

The eschatological vision of itself does not give sufficient content to what is truly human progress, but it does furnish some parameters for the discussion. As in much of Catholic moral theology, the content aspect comes in through the mediation of human reason. Human creativity and initiative are good and can participate and share in the work of creation, incarnation, and redemption. However, finitude, sin, and the lack of eschatological fullness, which in accord with the stance are three different aspects of reality, will always characterize the human enterprise in this world. Thus in approaches to bioethics I would argue against the strictly future eschatology of Paul Ramsey[19] and the overly realized eschatology of Joseph Fletcher.[20] Ramsey's eschatology influences his negative view toward possible developments in biomedicine, while at the same time Fletcher's eschatology supports his overly optimistic willingness to baptize almost any possible development.[21]

The eschatological vision together with theological and philosophical anthropological considerations also provides some parameters for judging scientific and technological accomplishment. Recent advances in biomedicine testify to the great creativity of human knowledge, but at the same time serious questions are raised in the process. Such contemporary experience correlates with and confirms the eschatological perspective mentioned earlier.

The Catholic theological tradition has a somewhat ambivalent record with regard to science and its applications in technology. In theory the Catholic tradition has always expressed an openness to the findings of science. Catholic theology has proudly proclaimed that faith and reason can never contradict one another. The early scientists in the medieval times were philosophers and theologians. Think, for example, of Albert the Great and Roger Bacon. However, in practice there was often a suspicion and distrust of the sciences. Recall the problems which the Catholic Church had with Galileo, with evolution, with the use of historical criticism in interpreting the scriptures, with psychoanalytic theory, with Teilhard de Chardin. What should be the attitude of Catholic theology to science in general and to biomedical science in particular? On the basis of the eschatology and anthropology sketched above, science and the particular science of biomedicine should be seen as limited goods which unfortunately might be influenced and abused because of sin.

I agree with the basic thrust of the Catholic tradition with its acceptance of human reason and human knowledge. Through knowledge and its application we can come to a better understanding of the human and try to improve human existence. Reason is basically good, and the human creature's scientific progress is a very responsible use of our God-given powers. However, human science and technology are also finite, limited, and subject to the corrupting influence of sinfulness.

The scientific and its technological application constitute a limited good which cannot be identified with the totally human. The anthropological considerations developed above insisted that the human is more than the physical and the biological. The scientific is only one aspect of the human and can never be identified with the totally human. The limitations of the empirical sciences are illustrated by the fact that science cannot penetrate the heights and the depths of human existence. Empirical science can never totally know the meaning of human life, human beauty, human wonder, human love, and human pain. The empirically scientific is only one limited part of the human and consequently cannot be totally identified with the human.

The human moral judgment must consider, but also relativize, the particular aspects of any one science — the psychological, the sociological, the pedagogical, the hygenic, the eugenic, and so on. All particular perspectives are ultimately relativized in the light of the human judgment, which is the universal and ultimate judgment. In this imperfect world nothing is going to be perfect from every particular dimension. The empirically scientific is a limited good which can never be totally identified with the human, and any one particular science is even more limited. One possible future development in genetics, according to some but not all scientists, involves the cloning of human persons. It might, so some say, be possible to clone any number of people who will have the same genetic makeup. In other words, all these people would be genetically identical twins. Even if it were genetically possible to clone one thousand Einsteins or some other person who is acclaimed to be a superior person, just think of the psychological problems that it would create for these one thousand identical twins. Experience points out the psychological difficulties created for children of famous people or for identical twins. Just because something is possible and feasible from the perspective of genetics does not mean that it is good from other perspectives or from the total human perspective.

Recent experience and history testify to the abuses of biomedicine. Think, for example, of the immoral experimentation on human beings, especially Jews, under the Nazis in Germany. But abuse and sin are not limited by geography, race, nation, or culture. People in the United States were aghast to discover in the early 1970s that black men in Tuskegee, Alabama, who volunteered for experimentation involving syphilis were not given penicillin after that was acknowledged to be the accepted treatment for the disease.[22]

Questions posed by biomedicine have helped form the above understanding of eschatology, anthropology, and the recognition of biomedical science and technology as limited human goods which can be abused.[23] Since this essay recognizes a dialogical relationship between moral theology and biomedicine, it is now appropriate to illustrate how moral theology with such a general attitude to biomedical science approaches issues raised in biomedicine. The general understanding of biomedical science as a human good which is, however, limited and can be abused calls for a basic openness to biomedical science and to the technology which results from it. As already pointed out, such an approach does not castigate all biomedical science and technology as attempts to play God and as failures to accept human creaturehood. There are limits, and there are occasions when one must say No to such technological possibilities; but a critical openness should characterize our attitude to biomedical research and technology. Even in rejecting specific technologies and possibilities one should be careful to avoid the seemingly loaded and unnuanced charge of playing God. Particular reasons should be given why such technologies are truly not human.

In the United States the President's Commission for the Study of Ethical Problems in Medicine and Biomedical and Behavioral Research issued a report *Splicing Life* in response to a letter of June 20, 1980, from the general secretaries of the three major religious groups representing Protestants, Catholics, and Jews.[24] I think the tone of the letter was too alarmist and perhaps involved some overreaction. At the present time gene splicing in laboratories does raise some ethical questions, but this research does not involve the remaking of human beings. One should be alert to the future consequences, but at the same time futuristic dangers should not be used in an alarmist fashion. There is need for constant oversight and wariness, but the present work in splicing genes is not necessarily opening a Pandora's box or playing God.

However, the limited aspects of biomedical science and technology in relationship to the human can never be forgotten. From this relationship between biomedicine and the human it follows that at times the human must say No to what is biomedically or genetically possible. Perhaps the most obvious illustration of this relationship concerns the prolongation of dying through technological means. At times one can and should pull the plug on the respirator, for example, and allow the patient to die in peace. The human must always control the technological.

Human control over biomedical science and technology also comes to the fore in the question of priorities in our society. Both in terms of research and in terms of technology there are limits on what society should invest. There can be no doubt that scientific and genetic breakthroughs are very enticing, but even more important is the less dramatic but more significant need of people for preventive medicine and better access to health care. Health care as such is a much broader term than medical care, but in the United States too much stress has been put on the aspect of medical care and all that goes into it. Limited resources might be better used for general health care rather than for exotic technology which ultimately cannot affect that many people. In questions of priority in health care, the danger always exists of giving too much importance to the pursuit of scientific and technological breakthroughs and not enough to the more ordinary ways of caring for the everyday health needs of people.

Questions of priority within health care itself also raise questions about broader societal priorities in general. Biomedical advances are associated primarily with the first world and industrial countries. One can never forget that more important human problems on this globe deserve greater attention than biomedicine and genetics.

In this world sin affects and influences all reality. Some of the more dramatic effects of the power of sin were mentioned in terms of inhuman experiments. However, what Christian theology calls sin can exercise its influence in less dramatic ways ranging from arrogance to paternalism. All admit in theory that medical care as such exists primarily for the good of the individual. Ultimate decisions about medical care, therefore, should rest with the individual patient. However, the complexity of medical care is often such that the individual must rely heavily on the advice of the physician. The temptation is always present to use that knowledge in a controlling and paternalistic way. Knowledge is power, and it can so readily be abused, often in very subtle ways. How often the doctor is tempted not to tell the patient everything because the doctor works under the impression that he or she knows best.

A subtle presence of sin (without necessarily imputing personal guilt to all involved) can often be detected in areas of experimentation as distinguished from therapy. Therapy exists for the good of the individual. Sometimes people will talk about experimental therapy because there is no assurance that the therapy will work, but such procedures still exist basically for the good of the individual patient. Experimentation is done not for the good of the individual but for the good of the human species, the good of knowledge, and the good of the particular science. In such experimentation there might be the danger of some harm to the individual. Medical ethics tries to safeguard the rights of the person undergoing experimentation through its insistence on informed consent. However, many pressures work against the real cooperation of volunteers with the researcher. Too often many people do not really distinguish between the doctor and the researcher. The temptation to be the first to achieve a scientific or technological breakthrough can very easily influence the way in which the experimenter proceeds. Contemporary bioethics has tried to deal with such problems through the establishment of committees to review and approve the experimentation that is being done. These review committees constitute a system of checks and balances that attempt to deal with the more subtle influence of human sinfulness.

The limitations of biomedicine and the danger of sinful abuse come to the fore in questions of positive eugenics. Until the present time most medical interventions have been done to overcome types of evil and human suffering. However, some now talk about genetics being able to make better human beings in the future. The recognition of both limitation and sinfulness call now for a critical questioning of these schemes. What constitutes a better human being? Are people with an IQ of 200 better than people with an IQ of 100? The means by which these proposals are to be carried out must also be subject to critical scrutiny. What about the mistakes and the mishaps that will occur in such experimentation? Dealing with human beings is entirely different from dealing with bacteria. If experiments on bacteria do not work, one can throw away the bacteria. One should never do that with human beings. If our genetic planners of the future are no better than public policy planners today, it seems that there will never be the rosy future that is sometimes portrayed.

Contemporary experience in biomedicine also calls to mind other aspects that fit under the categories of eschatology and theological anthropology — the tragic aspect of medicine and the ultimate basis for human dignity. Health-care professionals, scientists, and practitioners sooner or later recognize the tragic aspect of human existence and, to some extent, of their own profession.[25] Death is an inevitability in human existence, and all the knowledge and expertise available to human beings will ultimately be defeated by death. This experience merely confirms the eschatological recognition that the fullness of life will only come at the end of time. Christian eschatology and Christian life find their ultimate paradigm in the paschal mystery of Jesus. Through baptism Christians share in the dying and rising of Jesus. Through death itself we come to life. There is always a tragic aspect about death, but for the believer death is not the end but is the way to eternal life. Suffering, death, and the tragic dimension will color all of human existence, but for the Christian they are not the ultimate. They are penultimate realities that will be transformed in the fullness of life. The tragic will always be present in human existence, but it will never be the last word.

Biomedical science and technology exist to enhance human life and to attempt to alleviate some human suffering. The Christian attitude toward suffering must avoid the extremes of either thinking that one can overcome all suffering in this world or passively resigning oneself to do nothing in the face of suffering. Medicine has always experienced the tension of the Christian recognition of the tragic aspect of existence and the place of suffering. Biomedical science must try to do everything possible to alleviate human suffering, but it will never be totally successful. Especially in the plans and minds of some is a tendency to forget the limitations of biomedicine and the tragic aspect of human existence. Generally speaking, I prefer to avoid using the metaphor of playing God, but it is necessary to acknowledge the limits of biomedical science, the inherent limits involved in being human, and the tragic aspect of human existence.

Human beings can never have perfect control over their lives. The Planned Parenthood Association uses as an advertising slogan "Every child a wanted child." One can accept the concept of responsible parenthood and still question the slogan and the theory on which it is based. We human beings do not and cannot control all the realities that impinge on our lives. Life in fact would be very sterile and dull if everything could be totally planned in advance by ourselves. Because of their inherent limitations science and technology can never totally control human life. Experience shows that many things happen to human beings that they do not want and even try desperately to avoid. The whole of the Christian message holds out the possibility of redemption and hope in these difficult situations. Take, for example, the birth of a Down's syndrome child. No parent would want such a child. All can agree that science should do everything possible to eliminate Down's syndrome. However, for many people a retarded child has had a very redeeming effect in bringing out the best in all concerned. Experience shows that having such a child can also be a burden very difficult to carry. Christian eschatology reminds us that we cannot control all aspects of our lives, and in the process of human existence there will be suffering and pain. We try to do what we can to avoid suffering, but in the end we also recognize the redemptive power of God in Jesus that gives us hope.

Christian anthropology has always insisted, at least in theory, on a special care and concern for the blind, the lame, the weak, the deaf, the poor, and the oppressed. While striving to eliminate disease, human beings should never lose sight of the compassionate care that should be shown to all those who are less fortunate. There is a danger in a narrow technological perspective that efficiency is all important and those who are handicapped or less fortunate will not be accepted in a loving way. It is not inordinate for parents to pray for a healthy baby, but their desire must coexist with a care and compassion for the handicapped. Most people will admit that the humanity of a society is judged much more by its compassion and care for the handicapped and those in need than by its technological successes. As Christians we try to avoid suffering, but the tragic along with the possibility of redemption in its midst is always a significant reality in Christian life.

A further aspect of theological anthropology is closely connected with the above consideration. What is the ultimate reason of and basis for human dignity? Too often in an atmosphere in which efficiency, consumerism, and technology dominate, the value and dignity of the human person are based on what one does, makes, or accomplishes. The Christian perspective maintains that life is primarily a gift from God, and this giftedness is the basis of human dignity. Such a foundation for human dignity is ultimately connected with the Christian emphasis on the special care for the poor, the outcast, the handicapped, the lame, and the blind.

In health care and medicine the Christian perspective will always recognize and support the basic human dignity of the individual person, especially those who are weak and in need. A utilitarian methodology which is willing to sacrifice one or another individual for the greatest good is opposed to such a Christian understanding. So often today it is important to stand up for the rights of the individual, especially the weak and the unprotected. I think it is just such an attitude that is behind the Christian tradition's care and concern for the fetus. The Catholic tradition has always recognized that its position about the beginning of human life is a reasonable position. Rational arguments must be available to prove when human life begins, but these rational arguments will always be influenced by a Christian vision of special protection for the smallest and the weakest among us. It has already been pointed out that in experimentation and in consent situations the dignity of the individual must be protected.

An insistence on the human dignity, value, and rights of

the individual does not deny the social aspect of all human beings. The recognition that human beings are social by nature has been accepted within Catholic self-understanding. Society in the future may be faced with making difficult choices about not offering expensive life-prolonging technologies for its citizens. With only a limited amount of resources available society will have to make choices about what it can and cannot afford to do in providing health care. At the present time I hold that the social nature of human beings justifies parental consent for the use of children in experimentation when there is no discernible risk, even though the experimentation is not for the good of the individual children involved.

Moral theology in its dialogue with biomedicine has sharpened its own understanding of eschatology and the ramifications of this eschatological vision for evaluating human progress and for recognizing every particular science with its technological application as a limited good which can be abused. Eschatology also calls to mind the tragic aspect of all human existence and grounds human dignity in the gracious gift of God and not in the works and accomplishments of human beings.

IV. Discipline of Bioethics

A final important influence on moral theology has been the development and structuring of the discipline of bioethics. In the United States the growth of this discipline has been phenomenal. As might be expected, the effect of this new discipline on moral theology has been ambivalent. One positive aspect of the new discipline is the fact that it has put moral theology into dialogue with new partners, especially contemporary philosophy, medicine, law, sociology, and genetics. This dialogue can be most beneficial for moral theology. Until a few years ago philosophical ethics in the United States was not interested in content issues. Analytic and linguistic approaches dominated philosophy in general, while philosophical ethics stressed metaethical concerns. However, the number and significance of moral issues raised by biomedical advances have helped philosophy itself to realize the importance of these issues and the need to address them. Dialogue with contemporary philosophical approaches can and should contribute to the growth of Catholic moral theology. In addition to bringing moral theology into dialogue with contemporary philosophy, bioethics with its interdisciplinary approach also underscores the need for moral theology itself to have the same type of openness to interdisciplinary dialogue.

In the United States Catholic moral theology has been in sustained dialogue with Protestant Christian ethics. Many Protestants such as Paul Ramsey[26] have studied and critically related to what the Catholic tradition has historically proposed about such questions as prolonging life, solving conflict situations, and the nature of human parenthood. Protestants in turn have helped many Catholics both to appreciate and to renew their own tradition. Common discussion has solidified the close relationship between Protestant ethics and Catholic moral theology. In addition the concern with biomedical questions has also brought about a growing dialogue with Jewish ethics.[27]

However, there has been a significant negative effect on Christian ethics in the United States as a result of the development of the discipline of bioethics. One recent commentator has lamented the fact that theologians are no longer prominent in the area of bioethics. In the beginning of the discipline a few years ago theologians played a very prominent role.[28] I agree with this judgment that theology as such plays a lesser role in bioethics in the United States than it did a few years ago. As a result this new discipline might not be as helpful for the growth of Christian ethics in general and Catholic moral theology in particular as had been hoped.

What has happened? Many theological ethicists in the area of bioethics have paid less and less attention to the theological aspect of their ethics. Even some who claim to be doing theology do not often stress what is distinctive to the theological or Christian approach. The very structure of the discipline of bioethics has contributed to this situation. The problems being discussed are of great significance for society as a whole. Society is looking for ways of dealing with these questions through legislation, committees, and review boards. To communicate to the broader society it is better at times to prescind from any distinctive theological or faith position which is not shared by all the members of a pluralistic society. The purpose of much bioethical research is to serve the needs of society in general and thus shape how society responds to these problems. Bioethics has been funded by both private and governmental monies, but here again one has the impression that funding is more readily available if one prescinds from the faith differences existing among people in our country. In addition, the attention of bioethics is usually on particular cases or proposals for guidelines in specific matters. Many Catholic theorists have traditionally emphasized the role of reason in these areas and have not invoked distinctively Christian warrants. This factor also contributes to the fact that contemporary bioethics in the United States has not had a very positive influence on the development of Christian ethics or moral theology.

Some Christian ethicists such as James M. Gustafson[29] have been trying to emphasize more the theological dimension of bioethics. A greater theological output in this area is evident in the past year or so. At the very minimum it is important for theologians to discuss these issues from a theological perspective and thereby to develop the discipline of Christian ethics or moral theology.

Another significant ramification of the current development of bioethics concerns the distinction between the moral order and the legal order. Sometimes the literature itself needs to be more careful in making this distinction and in developing its position. A great difference exists between the moral order and the legal order, and different approaches and methodologies are involved.

The president's commission well illustrates the approach which is appropriate for law and public policy. In discussing various possibilities about proposed laws for determining the definition of death, the commission worked on the assumption that laws should stay as close as possible to the general feelings of people and should not be used as a means to bring about change in established attitudes. In defining death the commission's proposal retains the traditional criteria of the irreversible cessation of circulatory and respiratory functions but also adds another possibility — the irreversible cessation of all functions of the entire brain, including the brain stem.[30] Such a heavy reliance on contemporary attitudes is appropriate in determining public policy and law, but ethical methodology does not function in exactly the same way.

Contemporary Catholic moral theology in the area of bioethics has not given enough importance to this very significant distinction between the moral order and public policy. However, in its history Catholic theology has recognized this important difference. Thomas Aquinas explicitly dealt with the difference between the two orders and recognized that morality and legality are not the same.[31] In the light of our contemporary pluralistic society an even greater need is manifest to appreciate the difference between the two. In the twentieth century two very significant figures in the Catholic tradition, John Courtney Murray[32] and Jacques Maritain,[33] have also insisted on the importance of the distinction between the moral and the legal orders. Chapter nine will discuss in greater detail the distinction between the two orders. In the area of bioethics Richard McCormick has perceptively discussed this distinction in reflecting on his work as a member of the Ethics Advisory Board set up by the secretary of the then Department of Health, Education, and Welfare.[34] Continuing discussions in bioethics should encourage moral theology to study in an in-depth manner this important distinction between the moral and the legal orders. Thus in different ways the new discipline of bioethics is influencing moral theology.

This chapter has studied the effect of developments in biomedicine and in the new discipline of bioethics on moral theology. Four areas were discussed in some detail: historical consciousness, anthropology, eschatology and theological anthropology, and the dialogue with the developing discipline of bioethics. This study underscores the very historical nature of moral theology itself which is always trying to understand the issues of the present and its own self-understanding in the light of its historical tradition. The discipline grows and develops in and through its attempts to be faithful to its own tradition and to the signs of the times.

NOTES

1. Ethics Advisory Board, Department of Health, Education, and Welfare, *Report and Conclusions: HEW Support of Research Involving Human in Vitro Fertilization and Embryo Transfer* (Washington, DC: U.S. Government Printing Office, 1979).

2. David F. Kelly, *The Emergence of Roman Catholic Medical Ethics in North America* (New York and Toronto: Edwin Mellen Press, 1979).

3. Joseph F. Fletcher, *Medicine and Morals* (Princeton, NJ: Princeton University Press, 1954); Helmut Thielicke, *The Ethics of Sex* (New York: Harper and Row, 1964).

4. *Encyclopedia of Bioethics*, ed. Warren T. Reich, 4 vols (New York: Free Press, 1978).

5. For the commission's summary of its own work see President's Commission for the Study of Ethical Problems in Medicine and Biomedical and Behavioral Research, *Summing Up: Final Report on Studies of the Ethical and Legal Problems in Medicine and Biomedical and Behavioral Research* (Washington, DC: U.S. Government Printing Office, 1983).

6. Joanne Lynn, "Presidential Ethics Commission: Its Strengths, Weaknesses," *Hospital Progress* 64 (October 1983): 54-58.

7. Bernard Häring, *Free and Faithful in Christ*, vol. 1: *General Moral Theology* (New York: Seabury Press, 1978), pp. 28-58.

8. Daniel A. Cronin, *The Moral Law in Regard to the Ordinary and Extraordinary Means of Conserving Life* (Rome: Gregorian University Press, 1958).

9. Sacred Congregation for the Doctrine of the Faith, *Declaration on Euthanasia* (Vatican City: Vatican Polyglot Press, 1980).

10. Bert J. Cunningham, *The Morality of Organic Transplantation* (Washington, DC: The Catholic University of America Press, 1944).

11. Leroy Augenstein, *Come, Let Us Play God* (New York: Harper and Row, 1969).

12. Thomas Aquinas, *Summa theologiae*, $I^a II^{ae}$, prologue.

13. Bernard Häring maintains that the position favoring artificial

insemination with the husband's semen would find vast assent today. Häring, *Free and Faithful in Christ*, vol. 3: *Light to the World,
Salt for the Earth* (New York: Seabury Press, 1981), p. 25.

14. For a discussion of both sides of the question of norms see
Charles E. Curran and Richard A. McCormick, eds., *Readings in
Moral Theology No. 1.: Moral Norms and the Catholic Tradition* (New
York: Paulist Press, 1979).

15. For example, William E. May, *Human Existence, Medicine,
and Ethics* (Chicago: Franciscan Herald Press, 1977), pp. 82ff.

16. Karl Rahner, "Experiment: Man," *Theology Digest* 16 (1968):
57-69.

17. President's Commission for the Study of Ethical Problems
in Medicine and Biomedical and Behavioral Research, *Defining Death*
(Washington, DC: U.S. Government Printing Office, 1981).

18. Pope Pius XII, "Address to the International Congress of
Anesthesiologists on November 24, 1957," *Acta Apostolicae Sedis* 49
(1957): 1031, 1032.

19. Paul Ramsey, *Fabricated Man: The Ethics of Genetic Control*
(New Haven, CT: Yale University Press, 1970).

20. Joseph Fletcher, *The Ethics of Genetic Control: Ending Reproductive Roulette* (Garden City, NY: Doubleday Anchor Books, 1974).

21. For a further elaboration of my critique of Ramsey with oc-
casional references to Fletcher see Curran, *Politics, Medicine, and
Christian Ethics: A Dialogue with Paul Ramsey* (Philadelphia: Fortress
Press, 1973), especially pp. 173ff.

22. James B. Nelson and JoAnne Smith Rohricht, *Human
Medicine: Ethical Perspectives on Today's Medical Issues*, rev. ed. (Min-
neapolis, MN: Augsburg, 1984), pp. 68ff.

23. For a spectrum of Christian attitudes toward science and
technology, including more radical and negative approaches than
that proposed here, see Roger L. Shinn, ed., *Faith and Science in
an Unjust World: Report of the World Council of Churches' Conference on
Faith, Science, and the Future*, vol. 1: *Plenary Sessions* (Philadelphia:
Fortress Press, 1980).

24. President's Commission for the Study of Ethical Problems
in Medicine and Biomedical and Behavioral Research, *Splicing Life:
A Report on the Social and Ethical Issues of Genetic Engineering with Human
Beings* (Washington, DC: U.S. Government Printing Office, 1982).

25. The tragic aspect of medicine has been developed in great
detail by Stanley Hauerwas, *Truthfulness and Tragedy: Further Investiga-
tions in Christian Ethics* (Notre Dame, IN: University of Notre Dame
Press, 1977), especially pp. 147-202.

26. Paul Ramsey's primary works dealing with medical ethics

are: *The Patient as Person: Explorations in Medical Ethics* (New Haven, CT: Yale University Press, 1970); *The Ethics of Fetal Research* (New Haven, CT: Yale University Press, 1975); *Ethics at the Edges of Life: Medical and Legal Intersections* (New Haven, CT: Yale University Press, 1978). For my appreciation and evaluation of Ramsey's work see Curran, *Politics, Medicine and Christian Ethics: A Dialogue with Paul Ramsey*.

27. Seymour Siegel, "Genetic Engineering," *Linacre Quarterly* 50 (1983): 45-55. *Linacre Quarterly* is the official journal of the National Federation of Catholic Physicians' Guilds, and Rabbi Siegel, a professor at the Jewish Theological Seminary of America, is a member of the editorial advisory board of this journal.

28. Mark Siegler, "Bioethics: A Critical Consideration," *Église et Théologie* 13 (1982): 295-309.

29. James M. Gustafson, *The Contributions of Theology to Medical Ethics* (Milwaukee, WI: Marquette University Press, 1975).

30. *Defining Death*, pp. 55-84.

31. *Summa theologiae I^a — II^{ae}*, q. 96, a. 2 and 3; *II^{ae} — II^{ae}*, q. 10, a. 11.

32. John Courtney Murray, *We Hold These Truths: Catholic Reflections on the American Proposition* (New York: Sheed and Ward, 1960), pp. 275-289.

33. Jacques Maritain, *Man and the State* (Chicago: University of Chicago Press, 1956), pp. 58-64.

34. Richard A. McCormick, "Bioethics in the Public Forum," *Milbank Memorial Fund Quarterly* 61 (1983): 113-126.

PART TWO

Moral Theology Looks at Our Society

5: Just Taxation in the Roman Catholic Tradition

The Roman Catholic theological tradition has had a long and continuing interest in questions of justice. In the modern era the papal and hierarchical social teaching beginning with Pope Leo XIII's encyclical letter *Rerum novarum* in 1891 has developed into what is often called the social doctrine of the church. On the American scene the recent involvement of the American Catholic bishops in the pressing issues of peace and the economy has not been something totally disconnected with the Catholic tradition. Moral theology has been an important discipline in Catholic theology, and great attention has been paid to questions of justice. The moral theologians of the sixteenth and seventeenth centuries wrote large tomes commenting on questions of justice and rights. Questions involving the economy were not ignored by the tradition, as exemplified in the controversy that developed about usury and the morality of taking interest on loans.[1] In the light of this context one would expect that the Roman Catholic tradition has paid great attention to a fair distribution of the tax burden. In reality, however, very little has been written on a just system of taxation.

I. An Overview of Catholic Teaching on Just Taxation

The Scholastic and manualistic theologians from the fifteenth century onward did discuss the morality of taxation. Many of these theologians were well aware of the specific types of taxes which existed in their own territory. Louis Molina, for example, discussed the peculiar types of taxes existing in sixteenth-century Lusitania (basically present-day Portugal).

93

However, Molina and others said very little about the justice involved in a proper distribution of the tax burden among the people.[2]

John deLugo (d. 1660) was one of the best-known theologians of his day and dealt with the question of taxation in a way that is typical of the approach of the other manualists.[3] DeLugo devoted an entire disputation to the question of taxation and divided that discussion into eleven different sections which covered sixty-five long pages in his collected eight volumes on moral issues. The main focus of his discussion is the moral obligation to pay just taxes and who should be immune from that obligation. Section two deals with the question of a just distribution of the tax burden in discussing the three conditions, in addition to the necessary authority to levy taxes, that are required for a just tax. The first condition is there must be a just cause which is determined by the needs of the common good and not by the private good of the ruler. Second, there must be a proportion between the tax demanded and the cause for which it is demanded, for there is a danger that through excessive taxation the state itself can be destroyed. The third condition requires a geometric proportion in imposing the tax to be paid. If the cause for which the tax is needed pertains only to a few, the burden in the first place belongs on these few. However, if the primary beneficiaries of the tax are not able to bear the whole burden, then some tax can be required of all others because the members of the body ought to help one another. If for a common cause or necessity the tax revenue is needed, then all should be taxed equally, but based on an equality of geometric proportion, so that those who have more should pay more and those who have less should pay less. The common burdens should be distributed equally by a formal equality not by a material equality which in the end is the greatest inequality. In explaining this third condition this paragraph has paraphrased in a complete manner all that deLugo said on the question.

DeLugo goes on to raise one very important question about the justice of distributing the tax burden — Should taxes be placed on the common necessities of life — bread, wine, oil, meat? This question has been discussed at great length by earlier authors in the tradition of Roman Catholic moral theology. Many think that such taxes are unjust because the poor are burdened more than the rich. Many other authors exempt such taxes from injustice because of a number of different reasons often involving possible problems and inconveniences for society as a whole. DeLugo prefers that the tax be put on luxury items and not on other things that are necessary for ordinary life.

For all practical purposes deLugo in this comparatively long discussion says nothing else about the just distribution of the tax burden among the people. The seventeenth-century situation obviously differed from ours in many aspects of taxation. Recall how late it was that income taxes were levied in the United States. The problem of a just tax distribution was not as acute as it is today. But there is another very significant factor influencing the approach taken by deLugo and all the manualists. The manuals of moral theology had a very selective and narrow purpose — to train confessors as judges in the sacrament of penance. Their primary focus was on the rightness or wrongness of particular actions, the degree of culpability involved in such actions, and the obligations that the confessor had to impose on the penitent. It was only natural that such a literary genre would give primary attention to the obligation of paying the tax. Over the years a great dispute existed in the Catholic tradition about the moral obligation to pay just taxes. Is there such a moral obligation? If so, what is the nature of the obligation? What types of justice are involved? Is the person who defrauded or cheated at paying taxes held to make restitution? These concerns were the primary focus of the discussion on taxes in the manuals of Catholic moral theology.[4] This way of looking at the moral issues involved in taxation became for many the only approach. For example, the article dealing with taxation and justice in the recent *New Catholic Encyclopedia* is entitled "Taxation and Moral Obligation."[5]

However, in addition to the manuals of moral theology a genre of social ethical literature evolved especially in connection with the papal social teaching beginning with Pope Leo XIII in the late nineteenth century. This literature discussed the understanding and role of the state. Often this literary genre was in the form of commentaries on the official papal teaching, but the revival of Thomism at the same time also encouraged other Catholic philosophers and theologians to write significant studies and monographs on the state as well as on the social, political, and economic orders. This literary genre naturally considered the issue of taxation, but here too almost universally the authors stressed the moral obligation of paying taxes in our modern world and took exception to the more lenient position which had often been proposed in the manuals of moral theology. In addition this type of literature also discussed briefly the justice of tax distribution, often insisting on distributive justice as the criterion for determining the justice of taxation.[6] The writings of John A. Ryan, the foremost American Catholic social ethicist in the first half of the twentieth century, well typify this approach. Ryan insists on the moral obligation to pay just taxes based on commutative justice.[7] Although Ryan has no systematic discussion of taxation as such, his works do deal with just distribution of the tax burden under the rubric of distributive justice. John Ryan stresses that distributive justice calls for a proportional equality and a progressive tax on income and inheritance. In 1909 Ryan called for a heavy tax on the increased value of land.[8] In the social ethical tradition in Catholic theology in this century the justice of taxation has not been a burning issue, and the authors generally agreed that the common good and distributive justice formed the criteria for judging the justice of distributing the tax burden on the basis of proportional equality.

Official Roman Catholic social teaching since Leo XIII has discussed many significant moral issues facing society, but one is surprised to see how seldom the issue of tax justice has been addressed. John Cronin, summarizing and explaining the official Catholic teaching, observed that papal treatment of taxation is not extensive.[9] Leo XIII in *Rerum novarum* warns that public authority would act unjustly if it uses confiscatory taxes to destroy property rights.[10] Pius XI insists that the state take measures to make sure that the wealthy who possess more than their share of capital resources contribute to the primary needs of the common welfare.[11] Pope Pius XII devoted one entire address to the justice of taxation and insisted on the need for proportional taxes. The pope points out that modern states rightly have taken upon themselves more services and interventions, but taxes should not be so heavy as to oppress private initiative, check the development of industry and commerce, and work to the detriment of good will.[12] Pope John XXIII in *Mater et magistra* again stresses the importance of making tax burdens proportional to the capacity of the people contributing, but only three sentences of the long encyclical are devoted to taxation.[13] One looks in vain for any sustained treatment of taxation in the Pastoral Constitution on the Church in the Modern World or in later papal documents. Pope Paul VI in *Populorum progressio* raises the rhetorical question of whether we as individuals are ready to pay higher taxes so that public authorities can intensify their efforts on behalf of development.[14] The Second General Assembly of the Synod of Bishops mentions a graduated taxation of income in a consideration of the transfer of wealth from richer countries to developing nations.[15] Pope John Paul II in a very short address to fiscal counsellors points out three values that must be present in a just tax system and in just fiscal policies— equity, freedom, and the common good.[16]

Since 1966 the United States Catholic bishops have addressed a great number of pressing social, economic, and political issues. Many people today are familiar with the involvement of the American Catholic bishops on the issues of war and the economy. However, J. Brian Benestad and Francis Butler edited a five-hundred page book containing the statements of the United States Catholic bishops on the political and social order from 1966 to 1980.[17] The issues addressed are many and varied—political responsibility; peace and war, especially in relationship to Southeast Asia, the Middle East, and other troubled spots; SALT II and the Panama Canal treaties; development issues, including population and food questions; human rights and their application and acceptance throughout the world; domestic issues such as abortion, crime and punishment, capital punishment, poverty and welfare legislation, health insurance, the economy, family life, housing, immigration; labor issues especially in terms of migrant labor; discrimination against blacks and other minorities; problems of the rural areas, especially the family farm. Notably absent from this long and varied list are taxation and tax reform. Within their other statements there are occasional and passing references to a just tax system. In discussing the economy, for example, the bishops simply state that a just and equitable system of taxation requires assessment according to ability to pay.[18]

Although the justice of the tax system has not been discussed in any systematic way either in the theological or ethical literature on the one hand or in official Catholic teaching on the other, there has been on the contemporary church scene considerable discussion about other aspects of taxation. Tax exemption of church property and tax credits for private schools have frequently been mentioned. In the last few years there is a growing literature on tax resistance as a form of protest about the use of tax money, especially for military expenditures.

This overview has pointed out the lack of an in-depth, systematic discussion of the justice of taxation in both the theological literature and in the official Catholic teaching. However, general agreement exists about the broad outlines of a just tax structure. The criteria and principles of the common good, distributive justice, and proportionality have all been mentioned. It is important to ground these principles and understand them in a more systematic and reflexive manner so that they can be more adequately applied to the contemporary scene.

II. Relevant Considerations for Developing a Catholic Understanding of Tax Justice

The general Catholic position on a just distribution of the tax burden is basically grounded in three important realities — the nature, purpose, and function of the state; distributive justice; and the destiny of the goods of creation. In addition to having a full picture of how the Catholic tradition should approach the question of the justice of taxation, it is important to keep in mind the historical reality of the tithing system, the importance of making sure that the state recognizes its obligation to the poor, and what the Catholic tradition did say about the moral obligation to pay taxes. This section will briefly consider all these different relevant aspects in trying to develop more systematically a Roman Catholic approach to just taxation.

Nature of the State

The Roman Catholic tradition has insisted that the state is a natural society, for human beings are by nature social and called to live together in political society and in the state.[19] Human persons form the state to achieve those things for their own good and fulfillment which they could not achieve if they lived outside political society. The Catholic position thus differs from those theological traditions which see the state based on sin, with the primary negative purpose of keeping sinful human beings from destroying one another. In the Catholic understanding the state is a natural society with a positive function in pursuit of the good and is not characterized primarily in terms of coercion. Thomas Aquinas emphasized both the natural and positive aspects of the state by maintaining that even before or without the fall there would have been the state and political society.[20]

Traditionally the Catholic understanding of the state has seen itself as a middle position between the two extremes of individualism and collectivism. Individualism does not give enough importance to the social nature of human beings and the positive role of the state in helping individuals. Collectivism on the other hand does not give enough importance to the individual and the rights of individuals. The goal or purpose of the state in the traditional Catholic understanding is the common good. The Pastoral Constitution on the Church in the Modern World of Vatican II describes the common good as the sum of those conditions of social life which allow social groups and the individual members relatively thorough and ready access to their own fulfillment.[21] The goal of society is not the total aggregate of individual goods as in individualism or merely the public good of the whole as in collectivism. Human society is unique because it is a whole made up of other wholes. There is a reciprocal and even somewhat paradoxical relationship between the individual and society. According to Jacques Maritain a tension is present between the person as person and the person as individual. The person as person is a whole, and the common good of temporal society flows back on the person as person who transcends society. On the other hand the person as individual or part remains inferior to and subordinate to the whole. In such a way the Catholic tradition has tried to avoid the Scylla of individualism and the Charybdis of collectivism. Living in temporal society and in the state is primarily understood or experienced not as a coercive restriction of the freedom of the person but as a way to achieve one's own fulfillment as a social being and a human person.[22] Individualistic understandings of the role of the state see the promotion and safeguarding of individual freedom as the primary and only goal of the state. Collectivistic approaches stress the primacy of justice and downplay freedom. The Roman Catholic tradition with its emphasis on both the personal and the social has rightly insisted on the need for both freedom and justice.

In assigning proper roles to the person, intermediate groups, and the state, Catholic social thought stresses the principle of subsidiarity according to which individual persons and smaller intermediate groupings should be allowed and encouraged to do all they can for the common good. The state exists as a help (*subsidium*) to do what individuals and the smaller groups cannot do. However, recent official Catholic social teaching has recognized the increasing complexity and socialization of modern life, because of which the state must play an ever-increasing role in human affairs. Recall that Pope Pius XII recognized the growing role of the state in discussing taxation.[23] Pope John XXIII in *Mater et magistra* pointed out that in the contemporary context "it is requested again and again of public authorities responsible for the common good, that they intervene in a wide variety of economic affairs, and that, in a more extensive and organized way than heretofore, they adapt institutions, tasks, means, and procedures to this end."[24] The pope explicitly mentioned the need for state intervention to reduce imbalances, to keep fluctuations of the economy within bounds, and to provide effective measures for avoiding mass unemployment.

The state in the Catholic understanding plays a limited role, since there are many other groups and institutions which make up the broader society. Jacques Maritain distinguishes between the body politic and the state. The body politic is the whole of which the state is a part, but it is the part which specializes in the interest of the whole, namely, the common good. Familial, economic, cultural, educational, and religious life matter to the body politic as much as the strictly political life. Maritain's distinction is thus in keeping with the traditional Catholic emphasis on the limited role of the state. The state stimulates, coordinates, directs, and guides all others in working for the common good.[25]

The pursuit of the common good justifies the state's need for taxation to pay for necessary expenditures. However, taxation by its very nature today has many important effects on different aspects of the common good, all of which must be taken into account. Johannes Messner sees the principle of the common good in tax and fiscal budgetary policy affecting economic productivity, the economic order generally, the social order, and even cultural tasks. Thus, for example, as mentioned in summarizing the papal teaching, the taxation policy cannot be confiscatory or cannot unfairly and unnecessarily limit economic growth.[26] However, economic growth can never be seen as an absolute or the only factor involved. Taxation must also respond to the demands of distributive justice.

Distributive Justice

The Catholic tradition's approach to justice like its approach to the understanding of the state both is rooted in the Thomistic tradition and attempts to give due importance to both individual and social aspects. The different types of justice depend on the different types of relationships which exist.[27] Commutative justice governs the relationships existing between one individual and another. Legal justice directs the relationship of individual members to the social whole. Distributive justice regulates the relationship of the social whole to the individual. Recall that the individuals concerned in the last two types of justice are members of the social whole and should not be considered as outside of or opposed to the whole. Also, the social whole includes the state but also involves the wider reality which Maritain calls the body politic. In addition, commutative justice governs not only transactions involving two different individuals as when Mary buys something from Joan but also situations involving what might be called moral or juridical persons such as corporations or institutions.

Commutative justice is justice in the strictest sense of the term. Here the two persons are adequately distinct. In this case there is a debt in the very strict sense of the term. If I have bought an automobile, it already belongs to me. If I have stolen a TV set, the set now belongs to the rightful owner and not to me. Commutative justice involves a strict arithmetic equality which is totally independent of the persons involved and depends solely on the thing itself. If I borrow five dollars from you and five dollars from the richest person in the world, the debt in both cases is five dollars. Commutative justice considers just the thing itself and not the person. In this sense commutative justice is truly blind.

The Catholic tradition has recognized that the justice of taxation belongs to the realm of distributive justice, which is not justice in the strict sense. Distributive justice falls short of the perfect verification of justice found in commutative justice. In distributive justice the two persons involved are not adequately distinct, since the individual is a part of the social whole to which one is related. The individual does not have the same strict right to what is owed as in the case of commutative justice, for there the thing owed truly already belongs to the individual with the claim. What is owed in this case is determined, not by strict arithmetic equality, but by what Aquinas called geometric equality or what is commonly called proportional equality. Distributive justice is not determined merely by things themselves but necessarily and intrinsically involves a consideration of the person. Distributive justice is not blind, for distributive justice must take the person into account.

Distributive justice directs the relationship of the social whole and the state in the distribution of the goods and burdens that are part of communal existence in human society and in the state. The very general criterion governing distribution is that goods or advantages are to be distributed according to needs and necessities, while burdens should be distributed according to capacities. Those who are called upon to fulfill certain functions in the government of the state should have the ability to properly carry out their designated civil functions. The justice of the distribution of taxation should be in accord with the capacities of the individual to pay. On the basis of proportional equality and the relationship one's wealth and capacity to pay taxes, outstanding figures in the Catholic social ethical tradition, for example, Taparelli d'Azeglio and John A. Ryan, have argued for a proportional and progressive tax structure.[28] The rich should pay a greater percentage of their income and wealth for taxes. In more recent times the Catholic tradition has thus interpreted distributive justice and proportional equality as calling for a progressive or graduated tax. Unlike contemporary tax philosophers, Catholic thinkers today generally understand proportional equality as requiring a progressive tax structure. In the United States sales tax and social security taxes are two examples of taxes that are not progressive. Theoretically the American income tax is a progressive tax, but in reality so-called loopholes work against the progressive nature of the income-tax structure. A proportional distribution of the tax burden based on the ability to pay is the ethical criterion that should govern. However, such taxation cannot be confiscatory, nor should it work against the common good's interest in a fair economic productivity and distribution.

The Social Destiny of the Goods of Creation

The proper distribution of the tax burden can rightly be understood only in the wider context of the just distribution of the goods of creation in general. The Catholic tradition supports the basic principle that the goods of creation exist to serve the needs of all. Here again it is important to recognize how this understanding attempts to avoid the two extremes of individualism and collectivism. Individualism absolutizes private property and puts no limits on the right to own and to use private property. The collectivist tradition in its extreme form denies private property at least in terms of the ownership of the means of production. The Catholic tradition recognizes a right to private property, but this right is limited and not absolute.

Recent hierarchical church teaching has strongly emphasized the universal destiny of the goods of creation to serve the needs of all. Pope Paul VI in *Populorum progressio* cites the Second Vatican Council's statement that God intended the earth and all that it contains for the use of every human being and people. Paul VI draws the conclusion, "All other rights whatsoever, including those of property and of free commerce, are to be subordinated to this principle. . . . It is a grave and urgent social duty to direct them to their primary finality."[29]

How are the goods of creation to be distributed within a society in accord with this primary finality to serve the needs of all? Again distributive justice comes into play. In general, distributive justice in the Catholic tradition calls for the goods to be distributed with a heavy emphasis on need. John A. Ryan mentions five different canons for a just distribution of the products of industry — equality, need, efforts, productivity, and scarcity. Ryan himself proposes a sixth canon — human welfare, which includes all the others but puts a heavy emphasis on need as a basic floor upon which everything else builds. Different types of goods are to be distributed among the members of society. The goods to be distributed within society correspond with the rights of the members of society. There are different types of rights that have different types of bases. One who buys a one-year warranty for an appliance has the right to have that appliance serviced by reason of the contract that has been purchased. Fundamental human rights are based on the dignity of the human person and society's obligation to respond and protect that dignity and those rights. The right to life is thus a basic human right which society must protect. In terms of the economic goods of society and the products of industry a person has a right to that measure of external goods which is necessary for living a basically decent human existence. Distributive justice must recognize the needs of human beings to have what is necessary to live this minimally decent human life. Human needs thus give a right to this basic floor, but there are other aspects which enter into the broader question of the total distribution of the goods of creation.[30]

Note again that the Catholic approach finds a middle way between individualism and collectivism. Society as a whole does have a responsibility toward its members. Sheer individualism would not recognize any direct obligation beyond what is for the individual's own good. Collectivism would demand an absolute equality among all. It is interesting to note that distributive justice in the Catholic tradition has never demanded total equality. Distributive justice recognizes the need for a basic minimum for all but beyond that allows for inequality for various reasons. Likewise, distributive justice by opposing confiscatory tax policies protects the legitimate rights of the individual taxpayer. If anything, the Catholic tradition could be criticized for not spelling out in greater detail how and why such differences can be allowed above and beyond the basic minimum. Distributive justice consequently differs from equalitarian justice precisely because it does not demand total equality in external goods.

The traditional Catholic teaching going back to the very beginning insisted on the obligation of the rich to give to the poor. In medieval times some insisted that the obligation to give of one's superfluous goods was an obligation of justice. The individual had a right to keep for oneself not only what was necessary for decent human living but also what was required to live in accord with one's state in life, but what was then left over or superfluous had to be given to the poor.[31] Brian Tierney maintains that according to the canonist Johannes Teutonicus the obligation to give to the poor could be legally enforced. The poor person could denounce the offending rich person to the church, which could compel the rich to give to the poor through church censures and even excommunication as a last resort.[32] The medieval society in many ways was very unequal with a significant hierarchical ordering, but there was an insistence on the need for a basic minimum for all. In the present century official Catholic social teaching has given greater importance to equality, but distributive justice still does not call for equal shares of the world's economic goods for all.

In the contemporary understanding there is a social duty to redirect created goods to serve their primary finality of being for all. The state through its taxing system can and should work to help achieve this goal. Redistribution of wealth and income is thus a legitimate goal of taxation in particular and of the function of the state in general.

The Tithes

In addition to Catholic theory about the common good, distributive justice, and the social duty to redirect the created goods to their proper finality, there is an aspect of the Catholic tradition that at least deserves mention in the context of a discussion of the justice of taxation from the Catholic perspective. The issue of tithing has received considerable attention over the years but also has occasioned many polemical remarks. Based on the testimony of many experts, the view of an outsider is that the definitive history of the institution of tithing has not been written.[33] Problems abound in attempting to discover the true picture of tithing. The obvious sources are the writings of the patristic era and especially the legal writings and historical documents from the medieval period. However, there appears to have existed great differences in different parts of the world with regard to tithing. Also the legal writing does not necessarily reflect what was actually happening. In addition, all sides seem to recognize that there were some abuses connected with tithing and the control of church property. One has the feeling that both polemicists and medievalists who are working in the area of tithing can tend to overexaggerate its importance. Although recognizing the temptation to exaggerate, Giles Constable concludes that no tax in the history of Europe can compare with the tithes in the length of duration, extent of application, and weight of economic burden.[34]

For the purpose of this article it is important to point out that tithing was a tax and not simply a voluntary church offering. In religious circles today tithing is a voluntary offering. Most Americans rightly think of churches as voluntary societies whose members willingly contribute to the needs of the church. However, the early church and especially the medieval church were truly governments set up to regulate life in the spiritual sector just as there was a state government to take care of life in the temporal realm.

Tithing in the Christian church was based on the Hebrew scriptures, but there was no unified view of tithing in these scriptures themselves. There is little knowledge about the existence of tithes in the first four centuries. By the fifth and sixth century tithes were well established in the older parts of Christianity in the West. The earliest conciliar texts come from Merovingian Gaul in connection with the Council of Tours in 567 and the Second Council of Macon in 585. There is debate as to the observance of the law of tithes at these times, but it seems that tithes at least in some places were paid as a matter of course. The church law was thus observed. In the eighth century Pepin and Charlemagne provided civil enforcement of the obligation of paying tithes. All acknowledge that abuses gradually become more prevalent, but the extent of the abuses is debated. Churches and their revenues were given over to nobles and other lay people, who then could profit from these revenues. The Gregorian reform in the eleventh century and the canonical reform in the twelfth century attempted to renew the life of the church in all its aspects, including finance and tithing. For some time this renewal was successful, but after the thirteenth century tithes more and more lost their character as an income tax due to the church and became payment for property which was due to the lord who could be either civil or ecclesiastical.[35]

Many significant questions are involved in coming to a better understanding of tithes. Who had to pay tithes? At one time it seems that in general all paid tithes, but exemptions were customarily given especially to clerics and monks. On what goods were tithes paid? Carolingian legislation insisted that tithes be paid on all income, but often this seemed to be applied only to the fruits of agriculture. Also much discussion arises over the question of to whom the tithes were paid The ideal seems to be that tithes were paid to the parish church in which the sacraments of baptism and eucharist were celebrated, but often tithes went to bishops, monasteries, and even to absentee landlords. A fourth question concerns how the tithes should be used. Originally the care of the poor seems to have been the primary and fundamental use of tithes. Pope Zachary in 748 proposed a fourfold use of tithes — for the upkeep of the bishop, for sustenance of the clergy, for the building and repair of churches, and for the poor. In the Spanish system the poor were apparently not one of the beneficiaries of this particular revenue. Elsewhere the poor continued to be among those who received help from the tithes, but the division of the tithes that went to the poor was not necessarily one-third or one-fourth of the total.[36]

Any discussion of taxation in the Roman Catholic tradition cannot neglect the tithes, but for the purposes of this article the fragmentary evidence available does not say much to the question of a just distribution of the tax burden.

Distribution of Tax Revenue: Care of the Poor

A full and complete discussion of the justice of the tax burden requires at least a recognition of the fact that there is another side to the coin — the distribution of the funds administered by the state. An adequate consideration of government expenditures is obviously impossible to present in a few pages. However, from what has been said in the last two sections it is important to underscore that tax revenues and other state monies must be used to help the poor. Tithing itself was a tax with the purpose of helping the poor. Brian Tierney has written a fascinating small monograph on medieval poor law seen especially in the canonical theory and its practical application in medieval England particularly in the thirteenth century. In this context Tierney points out that the poor had a right to this type of help, and the intrinsic dignity of the poor person was to be respected at all times. The poor law was financed through the tithes as a tax. In addition to the tithes people were also encouraged to give alms.[37] As a medievalist Tierney recognizes the danger of overemphasizing what took place at that time, but he concludes that all in all the poor were better looked after in England in the thirteenth century than in any subsequent century until the present one. However, he hastens to make the reservation that such a statement is not saying much.[38]

The Catholic tradition in both its theory and practice has recognized that tax revenues should go to the help of the poor. Voluntary contributions alone are not going to meet the true needs of the poor. It would seem that such a conclusion is even more true in the midst of the social interdependence and complexities of our own age. The state should carry out its social function of redirecting the goods of creation to serve all God's people. The Christian tradition and the Christian

Church should stress this responsibility of society in general and of the state in particular for the care of the poor. Contemporary Roman Catholic theology has emphasized the option for the poor,[39] but one important way to carry out this option in the United States is to recognize the obligation of the state to insure that the poor have the minimum necessary for a decent human existence. One cannot discuss here all the aspects of the distribution of government funds, but the Catholic theological tradition must insist on the rights and needs of the poor to have their proper share of the goods of creation.

The Moral Obligation to Pay Taxes

For a complete understanding of the Catholic tradition's approach to justice and the distribution of the tax burden some consideration must be given to what was the primary concern in Catholic moral theology — the moral obligation to pay just taxes. A number of theories have been proposed in the Catholic tradition about the moral obligation of paying just taxes. A brief examination of these will also throw more light on the understanding of law and justice and how these two realities also affect the just distribution of taxes.

The most distinctive approach to the moral obligation of paying just taxes within the Catholic tradition was the penal-law theory. According to this theory no moral obligation exists to pay the tax, but there is a moral obligation to accept the penalty that may be imposed for not paying taxes. The purely penal law theory is a broad theory covering all civil law, which was often applied in the matter of paying taxes. According to Herron an interesting historical development is involved in the purely penal-law theory.[40] The theory goes back to the constitutions of religious orders and apparently appeared for the first time in the prologue of the Dominican constitutions in 1236. Henry of Ghent (d. 1293) was the first theologian to apply the theory to civil laws, but this theory was accepted and amplified by subsequent theologians such as the influential Suarez (d. 1617). Before the nineteenth century theologians understood a penal law to be one which does not command or prohibit something but which imposes a penalty on one for doing or omitting something (e.g., whoever does x must pay a penalty). However, since the nineteenth century theologians supporting the penal-law theory have also evolved their understanding of what is a penal law. Modern supporters of the penal-law theory understand a penal law to be based not on the wording of the law itself but on its obliging force. A penal law is one which morally obliges the person only to the penalty that might be imposed and not to the act itself which is forbidden or commanded. On the contemporary scene the vast majority of theologians reject this theory, but a minority still make a case for it.[41] However, one can with Herron remain unconvinced by the arguments proposed in favor of the merely penal-law theory but still accept that this theory on the basis of external authority is a probable opinion which can legitimately be followed in practice.[42]

It was only natural that theologians would tend to understand the law of paying taxes as a purely penal law. According to the historical study of Martin Crowe later theologians attribute the penal-law theory of taxation to Angelus of Clavisio (d. 1495) and Martin Aspilcueta (Doctor Navarrus, d. 1586). In retrospect it is not certain that later theologians held exactly what the earlier ones held, but the purely penal-law explanation of the tax obligation was widespread and often accepted in practice as a probable opinion that could be followed by the faithful even if the author personally gave little or no intrinsic merit to the purely penal-law theory.[43] A reaction developed against this theory in the twentieth century especially, in my judgment, by those who were writing in the context of social ethics and the mutual relationships between individuals and society. American authors such as Ryan and Land strongly opposed the purely penal-law theory of taxation and even appeared to be embarrassed by the fact that such a theory continued to exist in the Roman Catholic tradition.[44] However in contemporary practice some continue to maintain the possibility of a purely penal-law approach to just tax laws.[45]

The motivations behind such an approach are readily identifiable. Many of the tax levies in earlier times were unjust impositions made by kings and rulers for their own private needs and purposes. Most people did not take seriously the moral obligation of paying such taxes. The rulers themselves really did not care about the moral obligation of their laws. Recall too the primary literary genre of moral theology was the manual written for confessors to determine what was sin and what obligations the sinner had. The approach of this genre included a recognition that one could not demand more than was certainly obligatory of the individual penitent. Such authors were careful not to increase the sins of people by putting on them unnecessary and unworkable moral obligations. In this context the purely penal-law theory of taxation offered a helpful pastoral solution to the problem.

The purely penal-law theory of taxation solved important pastoral problems, while it created theoretical problems about the very meaning of law. Such a theory accepted a very voluntaristic and extrinsic notion of the obligation of law as coming from the intention of the lawgiver. However, the best of the Catholic tradition in following Aquinas understood the obligation of law as rational and intrinsic. In this tradition something is commanded because it is good and not the other way around. Law is an ordering of reason for the common good.[46] Especially in the late nineteenth and twentieth centuries Catholic theologians gave much more attention to social ethics and relationships within society and the state. The individual has an obligation to work for the common good. Consequently just tax laws morally oblige in conscience. Such an approach can still deal with the problem of abuse by recognizing that unjust laws by definition are not laws and do not oblige in conscience, although complications and problems exist in discerning what is an unjust tax law. In my view no rational basis exists for claiming that just tax laws do not oblige in conscience.

In the historical development before the nineteenth century the other position to the penal-law theory, which was sanctioned by St. Alphonsus (d. 1787) and the majority of theologians, held that just tax laws oblige in commutative justice. Recall that commutative justice involves one-on-one relationships. Crowe's historical study traces this theory back to St. Antoninus of Florence (d. 1449).[47] The theoretical basis for this position is a presumed contract or pact between the individual and the ruler or the state. The tax is the price paid by the subject or the citizen for the services rendered by the ruler and the state. Also some varieties of this implicit tax or covenant approach are put forth. Expenses legitimately incurred in the name of another must be borne by the other. The subjects or members of the community consequently have an obligation in commutative justice to repay the ruler or the community what was spent in their name.

A number of arguments could be proposed to show that no real contract exists in this case, but even more fundamentally the Catholic tradition does not want to use the metaphor of contract to understand the relationship between individuals and the state. Contractarian theories of the state are too individualistic, for they do not recognize that human beings are by nature called to live in political society. To live in a political society under particular rules is not something that individuals are free to do or not. Human beings are by nature social, and the social reality does not owe its existence to the free will of the contracting parties.

In my view the obligation to pay just taxes comes from the virtue of legal justice. This opinion was first proposed only in the middle of the nineteenth century, but it is now embraced by many theologians.[48] Legal justice governs the relationship between the individual and society or the state. The object of the virtue of legal justice is the common good. The individual member of political society and the state is morally obligated to work for the common good. The state needs tax money to provide for the common good, so the citizen is thus obliged in legal justice to pay just taxes. Why was this theory first proposed only in the midnineteenth century? Thomas Aquinas had spoken about legal justice but had not given great attention to it.[49] Subsequent Catholic theologians tended to neglect the concept of legal justice. From the midnineteenth century down to the present an increased interest in social ethics is evident. Pope Leo XIII, who helped spark this interest with his social encyclicals, also insisted on the importance of Thomistic philosophy and theology.[50] It was only logical that in such a context the Thomistic concept of legal justice would receive more importance. Today the majority of Catholic theologians understand the obligation to pay just taxes as based on legal justice.

For completion's sake a word should be said about social justice. The three types of justice — commutative, distributive, and legal — deal with three different types of relationships which exist in human society — one to one, society to the individual, and the individual to society. However, in the encyclical *Quadragesimo anno* Pope Pius XI introduced the term social justice that has often been used since that time. The problem arose as to the exact meaning of social justice and its relationship to the other three kinds of justice. Different theories have been proposed about social justice, but the more common position among Catholic ethicists sees social justice as identified with legal justice.[51] Chapter eight will show that the United States bishops in their pastoral letter on the economy understand social justice to be synonymous with legal justice.

In my view there is an obligation in legal justice to pay just taxes. Unjust taxes do not oblige in conscience, but this paper cannot delve more deeply into the question of how and by whom the injustice is discerned. This consideration fills out the basis for understanding and appreciating what the Catholic tradition brings to a proper understanding of justice in relation to the tax burden.

III. Conclusion

The second section of this study has attempted to flesh out the basis for a more systematic and in-depth understanding of the approach to a just distribution of the tax burden in the Roman Catholic tradition. This analysis has not contradicted the rather summary statements on tax justice which have been made in the past but rather serves to give them a more secure grounding in the Catholic tradition.

The Catholic tradition highlights the importance of the following aspects in arriving at a just distribution of the tax burden — the universal destiny of the goods of creation to serve the needs of all God's people; the role of the state in working for the common good with a recognition of the growing complexity of social relations calling for an increased role of the state; a notion of distributive justice with an emphasis on the criterion of ability or capacity as the principle to govern the tax burden; the need for the state to promote the rights of the poor to share properly in the goods of creation.

In this light the following goals should govern tax policy. Taxation should serve the common good and thus can be used to promote certain activities which promote the common good. Distributive justice calls for a proportionate and progressive distribution of the tax burden. Thus taxation is one way in which the state can work for a more just distribution of the goods of this world. In terms of serving the common good, taxation must promote just economic growth and the prosperity of the nation, but in our interdependent world the prosperity of the nation is intimately linked with the whole world.

The goals of a just tax policy in my judgment are consequences of the considerations developed in the second part of this study. However, some within the Catholic tradition might disagree with my interpretation of the goals mentioned above. In the last few years in the United States criticism of the social teachings proposed by the American Catholic bishops has come from authors such as Michael Novak and J. Brian Benestad among others.[52] These critics in general disapprove of the bishops' position on social issues as being too "liberal," while they themselves espouse what is often described as "neoconservatism."

A different interpretation might stress the demands of the common good for economic growth and well-being as more important than distributive justice. In any possible conflict in my judgment the presumption is always in favor of the demands of distributive justice for a proportionate and progressive tax burden. The very acceptance of distributive justice means that the ultimate criterion cannot be the bottom line in the gross national product or the growth of the economy as a whole. Distributive justice insists on the need to make sure that the economic pie is fairly divided. The tax structures cannot be confiscatory and cannot take away incentives for economic development, but such goals should ordinarily be achieved without detriment to the demands of distributive justice.

A second possible disagreement concerns the role of the state in the distribution of wealth in society and in its care for the poor. As pointed out, Catholic teaching has insisted on the principle of subsidiarity, but more recent official Catholic teaching recognizes a greater role for the state in the light of the growing complexity and socialization of human existence. In the 1950s what little Catholic writing there was on the question of tax justice often expressed the fear of "statism."[53] Today the magnitude of these problems of wealth distribution and care for the poor requires state involvement. While stressing the need for an important role for the state, my position also recognizes the need for the cooperation of all concerned.

In the light of the goals of a just tax policy one can then criticize the existing tax structures and the contemporary attempts at tax reform. Evident is a growing discussion within this country about the need for tax reform, but the Catholic tradition has contributed very little. Ronald Pasquariello has written a short book and an article on unjust tax structures.[54] To its credit the National Conference of Catholic Charities has shown some interest in this question by adopting a "Policy Statement on Distributive Justice and Taxation" at its 1977 meeting and by publishing a short but perceptive article by Edward J. Ryle in its journal.[55]

To criticize fully the present tax structure or to propose a concrete tax-reform proposal lies beyond the scope of this paper. However, the goals proposed here at the very minimum raise serious questions about the existing tax structure. Some taxes that are heavily relied upon such as sales tax and social security tax are regressive and do not embody the principle of proportional and progressive taxation demanded by distributive justice. The greatly diminished role of corporation taxes raises serious questions about proper distribution. The progressivity of the individual income tax system has been reduced, with a concomitant shift in the tax burden from higher to lower- and middle-income taxpayers.

The focus of this chapter has been what the Catholic ethical tradition has to say to the question of a just tax structure. The first section indicated how little in-depth study has been done on this topic, even though there appears to be a generally accepted but not well-developed position within the Catholic tradition. The second part attempted to spell out in greater detail the basis for the generally accepted Catholic position. A third concluding section proposed the goals that should guide a just tax structure in accord with Catholic self-understanding

and briefly illustrated how these goals might affect some particular questions today.

NOTES

1. John T. Noonan, Jr., *The Scholastic Analysis of Usury* (Cambridge, MA: Harvard University Press, 1957).
2. Ludovicus Molina, *De justitia et jure opera omnia* (Geneva, 1759),
III, d. 665.
3. Johannes deLugo, *Disputationes scholasticae et morales* (Paris,
1869), VIII, d. 36, pp. 606-672.
4. Martin T. Crowe, *The Moral Obligation of Paying Just Taxes*
(Washington, DC: The Catholic University of America Press,
1944).
5. Charles E. Curran, "Taxation and Moral Obligation," *New
Catholic Encyclopedia* (New York: McGraw-Hill, 1967), XIII, pp.
950, 951.
6. John F. Cronin, *Social Principles and Economic Life*, rev. ed.
(Milwaukee: Bruce, 1964), pp. 257-259.
7. John A. Ryan, *The Catholic Church and the Citizen* (New York:
Macmillan, 1928), pp. 60-65.
8. John A. Ryan, "A Program of Social Reform by Legislation,"
The Catholic World 89 (1909): 432-444, 608-614; John A. Ryan, *Distributive Justice* (New York: Macmillan, 1916), pp. 101-117, 296-307.
9. Cronin, *Social Principles and Economic Life*, p. 257.
10. Leo XIII, *Rerum novarum*, par. 47, in Etienne Gilson, ed.,
The Church Speaks to the Modern World: The Social Teachings of Leo XIII
(Garden City, NY: Doubleday Image Books, 1954), p. 231.
11. Pope Pius XI, *Divini redemptoris*, par. 75, in Terence P.
McLaughlin, ed., *The Church and the Reconstruction of the Modern World:
The Social Encyclicals of Pius XI* (Garden City, NY: Doubleday Image Books, 1957), p. 396.
12. Pope Pius XII, "Address to the International Association
for Financial and Fiscal Law," *The Pope Speaks* 4 (1957-58): 77-80.
13. Pope John XXIII, *Mater et magistra*, par. 132, 133, in Joseph
Gremillion, ed., *The Gospel of Peace and Justice: Catholic Social Teaching
since Pope John* (Maryknoll, NY: Orbis Books, 1976), p. 172.
14. Pope Paul VI, *Populorum progressio*, par. 47, in ibid. p. 401.
15. Second Synod of Bishops, *Justitia in mundo*, par. 66, in ibid.,
p. 527.
16. Pope John Paul II, "Discours à des conseillers fiscaux," *La
Documentation Catholique* 78 (Jan. 4, 1981): 7.
17. J. Brian Benestad and Francis J. Butler, eds., *Quest for Justice:*

A Compendium of Statements of the United States Bishops on the Political and Social Order, 1966-1980 (Washington, DC: United States Catholic Conference, 1982).

18. Ibid., p. 265.

19. See, for example, Jacques Maritain, *Man and the State* (Chicago: University of Chicago Phoenix Books, 1956); Johannes Messner, *Social Ethics: Natural Law in the Western World* (St. Louis: B. Herder, 1965); Heinrich A. Rommen, *The State in Catholic Thought: A Treatise in Political Philosophy* (St. Louis: B. Herder, 1950).

20. Thomas Aquinas, *Summa theologiae* (Rome: Marietti, 1952), I, q. 96, a. 4.

21. Pastoral Constitution on the Church in the Modern World, par. 26, in Gremillion, *The Gospel of Peace and Justice*, p. 263.

22. Jacques Maritain, *The Person and the Common Good* (Notre Dame, IN: University of Notre Dame Press, 1966).

23. See note 12.

24. Pope John XXIII, *Mater et magistra*, par. 53-57, in Gremillion, *The Gospel of Peace and Justice*, pp. 154, 155.

25. Maritain, *Man and the State*, pp. 9-19.

26. Messner, *Social Ethics*, pp. 679-692.

27. For expositions of the approach to justice in the Catholic tradition see Joseph Pieper, *The Four Cardinal Virtues* (Notre Dame, IN: University of Notre Dame Press, 1966), pp. 43-113; Daniel C. Maguire, "The Primacy of Justice in Moral Theology," *Horizons* 10 (1983): 72-85. For a different understanding of legal justice see Jeremiah Newman, *Foundations of Justice* (Cork, Ireland: Cork University Press, 1954).

28. A. Perego, "L'imposta progressiva nel pensiero del P.L. Taparelli d'Azeglio," *La Civiltà Cattolica* 98, n. 4 (1947): 136-144; Ryan, *The Catholic World* 89 (1909): 610 ff.

29. Pope Paul VI, *Populorum progressio*, par. 22, in Gremillion, *The Gospel of Peace and Justice*, p. 394.

30. Ryan, *Distributive Justice*, pp. 243-253.

31. Hermenegildus Lio, *Estne obligatio justitiae subvenire miseris?* (Rome: Desclée, 1957).

32. Brian Tierney, *Medieval Poor Law: A Sketch of Canonical Theory and Its Application in England* (Berkeley: University of California Press, 1959), pp. 38, 39.

33. Catherine E. Boyd, *Tithes and Parishes in Medieval Italy* (Ithaca, NY: Cornell University Press, 1952); Giles Constable, *Monastic Tithes: From Their Origins to the Twelfth Century* (Cambridge: Cambridge University Press, 1964).

34. Constable, *Monastic Tithes*, p. 2.

35. Boyd, *Tithes and Parishes*, pp. 26-46; Constable, *Monastic Tithes*, pp. 1-55.

36. Constable, *Monastic Tithes*, pp. 31-56.

37. Brian Tierney, *Medieval Poor Law*.

38. Ibid., p. 109.

39. Donal Dorr, *Option for the Poor: A Hundred Years of Vatican Social Teaching* (Maryknoll, NY: Orbis, 1983).

40. Matthew Herron, *The Binding Force of Civil Laws* (Paterson, NJ: St. Anthony Guild Press, 1958), pp. 33-40.

41. For acceptance of the purely penal-law theory by contemporary theologians see Edward T. Dunn, "In Defense of the Penal Law," *Theological Studies* 18 (1957): 41-59.

42. Herron, *The Binding Force of Civil Laws*, p. 111.

43. Martin T. Crowe, *The Moral Obligation of Paying Just Taxes* (Washington, DC: Catholic University of America Press, 1944), pp. 28-42).

44. John A. Ryan, *The Catholic Church and the Citizen* (New York: Macmillan, 1928), pp. 47ff.; Philip S. Land, "Evading Taxes Can't Be Justified in Conscience," *Social Order* 5 (1955): 121-125.

45. E.g., John F. Dedek, "Taxation and the New Economics," *Chicago Studies* 12 (1973): 29-38.

46. Thomas E. Davitt, *The Nature of Law* (St. Louis: B. Herder, 1951).

47. Crowe, *The Moral Obligation of Paying Just Taxes*, pp. 42-72.

48. Ibid. pp. 72-82.

49. *Summa theologiae*, *II^a II^{ae}*, q. 58, a. 5, 6.

50. Pope Leo XIII, *Aeterni patris*, in Gilson, *The Church Speaks to the Modern World*, pp. 29-54.

51. William Feree, *The Act of Social Justice* (Dayton: Marianist Publications, 1951).

52. Michael Novak, *The Spirit of Democratic Capitalism* (New York: Simon and Schuster, 1982); J. Brian Benestad, *The Pursuit of a Just Social Order: Policy Statements of the U.S. Catholic Bishops, 1966-1980* (Washington, DC: Ethics and Public Policy Center, 1982).

53. E.g., R.C. Jancauskas, "Social Effects of Taxation," *Social Order* 6 (1956): 330-332.

54. Ronald Pasquariello, *Tax Justice: Social and Moral Aspects of American Tax Policy* (Lanham, MD: University Press of America, 1985); "A Jungle of Injustice: US Tax System Stands in Need of Overhaul," *National Catholic Reporter* 20 (February 17, 1984): 9-11.

55. "Policy Statement on Distributive Justice and Taxation," *Agenda for Action* (Washington, DC: National Conference of Catholic Charities, 1977), pp. 16-20; Edward J. Ryle, "Tax Justice as a 'Catholic Issue'," *Charities USA* 10 (November 1983): 10-12.

6: Filial Responsibility for an Elderly Parent

The topic of the moral responsibility and legal obligation of the family toward elderly parents is more complex than one might suspect at first glance. In the care for the aged many actors must be considered in order to recognize and understand the diverse responsibilities of each. In the first place there is the individual elderly person, who has the moral obligation to make some preparation for retirement and old age. Then the family members and a number of other organizations, many of a voluntary nature, take upon themselves the care for the aged. In addition there is the political society or the state, which in the United States exists on the federal level, the state level, and the local level. This chapter focuses on the moral and legal obligations of adult children to aging parents in the light of all these other factors. As will be illustrated again in the ninth chapter, the moral and legal orders are related but different.

1. The Present Situation

The logical starting place for our analysis is a description of the present situation with regard to the role of adult children in caring for aged parents. The first area to be considered in the present situation is the legal aspect of filial responsibility for an aged parent, especially in terms of financial obligations. The legal obligation of children to care for an aged parent was enshrined in the Poor Law of England from the end of the sixteenth century until the midtwentieth century. According to the famous statute of Elizabeth I in 1601, "The father and grandfather, and the mother and grandmother, and the children of every poor, old, blind, lame and impotent person, or other person not able to work, being of a sufficient ability, shall at their own charges, relieve and maintain every such poor person in that manner, and according to that rate as by the justices . . . shall be assessed."[1] The general opinion has been that this legal obligation represents the traditional teaching of Christianity and Western civilization (not that the two are identical) until recent times. However, such a judgment is wrong.

In the first place Elizabethan poor law itself was something new. Medieval poor law as enshrined in the canon law of the church took a different approach. As the last chapter pointed out, medieval poor law was financed through the tithes or the church tax. The poor had a right to assistance, and the intrinsic dignity of the poor was to be respected at all times. Assistance to the poor and the elderly among them was not conditioned upon no other financial help being available from family members. Brian Tierney in a monograph on medieval poor law has shown that the law was applied and lived in medieval England.[2] Tierney's conclusion, although quite modest, is startling in its contrast with the generally accepted position — the poor were better looked after in England in the thirteenth century than in any subsequent century until the present. However, Tierney adds the reservation that such a statement is not saying much.[3]

English Poor Law was incorporated into some state laws concerning care for the aged in this country, especially in those states that came out of a Puritan tradition. However, until the twentieth century the prescription on filial responsibility enshrined in these laws was not really tested. Society was structured in such a way that elderly parents were always assured of care. The family, especially on the farm, was an economic unit headed by the father with a privileged place for the mother. The situation changed dramatically with the advent of individually earned cash income, the industrial revolution, and the breakup of the extended family. In the light of these facts one cannot claim that until the present century the moral recognition of close family bonds insured that the aged and the elderly would be taken care of in the family; as the old saying goes, untested virtue is no virtue at all.[4]

In the beginning of the twentieth century the question of ethical choice in this matter arose for the first time for all practical purposes because the aged population increased, and fewer of the elderly controlled their own situations. Some did urge the legal obligation of adult children to care financially for aged parents. However, most western countries abandoned the legal enforcement of filial responsibility for the aged long before the United States. In 1965 Congress passed a law providing for Medicaid, medical care for all the poor including the aged poor, with the explicit condition that the states not require contributions from adult children. In 1973 the Old Age Assistance Program (OAA) was replaced by Supplemental Security Income (SSI) to aid the poor elderly, and no provision was made for filial contributions.[5]

However, a significant change occurred in February 1983. The Department of Health and Human Services released a special supplement to the state Medicaid manual maintaining that "the law and regulations permit states to require adult family members to support adult relatives without violating the Medicaid statute. . . . Such contribution requirements are permissible as a state option." According to the interpretation of the present Reagan administration such an option for the individual states does not violate the provision of the Social Security Act that prohibits a state Medicaid plan from considering the financial resources of relatives of persons cared for under Medicaid. To avoid violating the earlier provision of the law this interpretation insists that the individual states must require such financial support through a statute of general applicability and not as a part of the state Medicaid plan. In addition, the states cannot merely assume that the income of adult children or their family responsibility payments are available to the Medicaid recipient. The February 1983 regulations also insist that the states cannot deny Medicaid services to a person whose responsible relatives refuse to contribute to that person.[6]

The effect of these regulations involving this new interpretation remains uncertain. Some maintain that these regulations still go against provisions of the current Medicaid law and could and should be challenged in the courts. Only a very few states have passed such legislation, while the vast majority of the states have taken no action on this new possibility.[7]

After surveying the legal aspects of the question, our focus now shifts to the nature of the personal relationship existing between adult children and aged parents at the present time. Does the fact that the Medicaid law and the vast majority of the states do not require adult children to contribute financially to a poor aged parent mean that the relationship between adult children and their elderly parents has broken down? A recent government report points out that contrary to the myth that most older persons do not have contact with their children, the most recent data available shows that most elderly people live relatively close to at least one of their surviving children and that contact with such children is frequent. Four-fifths of older persons have one or more surviving children. According to the data taken in 1975 about 75 percent of the elderly with surviving children saw one or more of their children within the week prior to the survey, and only 11 percent had not seen an adult child in the previous month. Most elderly do not receive their primary personal relationships and human support from their adult children, but in general frequent contacts indicate the existence of good personal relationships.[8]

Perhaps some of the myths about deteriorating relationships between the elderly and their adult children come from the decreasing number of the elderly who are living with an adult child. It can reasonably be estimated that one in six aged persons shared a dwelling unit with an adult child in 1976. The proportion of the elderly living with an adult child has continually decreased in the last few decades. The proportion of the aged living with adult children was 30 percent in 1952, 28 percent in 1957, and 20 percent in 1968. However, the conclusion from this is not that the aged are being put into institutions. In 1966 about four percent of the aged were in institutions, but now only about five percent are institutionalized — a difference that can be wholly accounted for by the increased aging of the aged population itself. The situation of the number of institutionalized elderly people in the United States compares most favorably with the statistics from Great Britain, which has strenuously pursued a policy of discouraging institutionalization by providing many support services to keep the elderly at home. It is true that aged parents live with adult children more frequently among the poorer classes, which points out that often poverty or lack of money has much to do with this reality. Even in such living relationships it is not necessarily a one-way street with the adult children doing all the giving. An aged parent in the home can help with many of the chores involved in running a home. No doubt the vast majority of elderly people themselves prefer to live independently as long as they are able. In contrast with the past, elderly people have the opportunity from an economic viewpoint to live independently. One cannot conclude that children today are less loving toward aged parents because of the decline in the number of elderly living with adult children.[9]

In addition to general concern and relationship on the one hand and housing on the other, adult children can also help their aged parents through financial contributions. Surveys indicate that only a small minority of people in general and of the elderly in particular believe there is an obligation for adult children to contribute financially to elderly parents when all the obligations of these children are taken into account. The statistics on the actual practice of cash contributions to aged parents vary somewhat depending on what is regarded as a cash contribution: for example, gifts of various types, the provision of a car, rent, or clothing. However, it seems that only about two to three percent of the elderly receive direct cash contributions from their adult children. Cash contributions by adult children are not significant as a general pattern for the elderly.[10]

In summary, the contemporary situation has the following features. In almost all the states no legal obligation exists for adult children to contribute financially to an aged parent who is poor and in need. A declining rate of aged persons shares a dwelling unit with an adult child, but the figure of one of six elderly in this situation in 1976 in itself constitutes a significant number. Voluntary cash contributions by adult children to the elderly are not significant as a general pattern. However, the vast majority of the aged are in contact with and have relationships with their adult children.

II. Legal Enforcement of Filial Responsibility

Many aspects are involved in the question of filial responsibility toward an aged parent. The first aspect to be considered is that of a legally enforced financial responsibility of children for an aged parent. The previous chapter briefly discussed the role of the state in the Catholic tradition. This section will develop the proper understanding of the diverse roles and functions of the individual, the family, other voluntary associations, and the state itself.[11] In referring to the state as a genre, the Catholic social tradition has understood the one national political government and did not distinguish its subdivision into federal, state, and local levels as in the United States. Catholic social thought recognizes the state as a natural society grounded on the social nature of the human person. Human persons are by nature social and political and band together in political society to achieve the common good of society, which ultimately redounds to the good of the individual. Without political society the individual could not achieve the fullness of one's own existence. Such an understanding of the state differs from the Lutheran interpretation, which sees the state primarily as a response by God to sinful human beings, whereby through the power of coercion sinful people are kept in check and prevented from harming one another. In this conception the state owes its origin not to human nature itself but to human sinfulness, and its primary purpose is the negative one of preventing disorder rather than the more positive function of working for justice.[12]

As mentioned in the last chapter, the Catholic understanding tries to find a middle ground between an individualism which so stresses the individual that the social aspect is denied and a collectivism which so stresses the collectivity that individual human rights are denied. In this approach due regard is given to the individual, the family, and voluntary groups and organizations existing within the state. Catholic theology, with increasing vigor in the twentieth century because of the rise of totalitarianism, has insisted on certain basic, inalienable natural rights that belong to every human being by reason of one's humanity and must be recognized by all others and by the state.[13] The family is a natural society, the basic unit in the larger society, and has its rights independently of any conferral by the state. Although a natural society, the family is traditionally called an imperfect society precisely because of itself it is incapable of satisfying all the natural tendencies and demands of its members. The Catholic insistence on society as an organism emphasizes the importance of and need for intermediary groups between the family and the state. Finally, the state itself has the function of directing and guiding all to the common good.

What is the role of the state and its relationship to individuals, families, and voluntary associations in society? Pope Pius XI in the encyclical *Quadragesimo anno* enunciated the principle of subsidiarity which is deeply rooted in the Catholic theological heritage. The pope recognized that even at that time changed conditions meant that large groups had to do what previously was done by smaller groups, but Pius XI continued:

> Still, that most weighty principle, which cannot be set aside or changed, remains fixed and unshaken in social philosophy: just as it is gravely wrong to take from individuals what they can accomplish by their own initiative and industry and give it to the community so also it is an injustice and at the same time a grave evil and disturbance of right order to assign to a greater and higher association what lesser and subordinate organizations can do. For every social activity ought of its very nature to furnish help to the members of the body social and never destroy and absorb them. The supreme authority of the state ought, therefore, to let subordinate groups handle matters and concerns of lesser importance which would otherwise dissipate its efforts greatly. Thereby the state will more freely, powerfully, and effectively do all those things which belong to it alone because it alone can do them: directing, watching, urging, restraining as occasion requires and necessity demands. Therefore, those in command should be sure that the more perfectly a graduated order is preserved among the various associations, in observance

of the principle of "subsidiary function," the stronger social authority and effectiveness will be, and the happier and more prosperous the condition of the state.[14]

The principle of subsidiarity was enunciated in a negative and restrictive manner, and many Catholics have used the principle to argue against the increasing role of government especially in the wake of the Great Depression and the Second World War.[15] This historical context helps to explain why Pope John XXIII in *Mater et magistra* in 1961 strongly argued against a minimalistic interpretation of the principle of subsidiarity.[16] *Mater et magistra* occasioned a great reaction and even the first public dissent in contemporary American Catholic history from a papal encyclical. This dissent was concretized in the expression of William F. Buckley, "*Mater, si; magistra, no.*"[17] Pope John (par. 50) cites as the reason for writing a new encyclical in 1961 the need to resolve the social question in ways more in accord with the needs of the present time. *Mater et magistra* (par. 46) points out that contemporary circumstances have greatly changed in the twenty years preceding the encyclical. Under the heading of "Explanation and Development of the Teachings of *Rerum Novarum*," the encyclical (par. 53) recognizes the need for private initiative and then cites the principle of subsidiarity as proposed in *Quadragesimo anno*. Pope John XXIII (par. 54) then immediately adds that recent developments provide "reasons why, to a greater extent than heretofore, it is within the power of public authorities to reduce imbalances. . . . Consequently, it is requested again and again of public authorities responsible for the common good that they intervene in a wide variety of economic affairs, and that, in a more extensive and organized way than heretofore, they adapt insitutions, tasks, means, and procedures to this end." However, the pope again cautions that state intervention must respect the basic rights of each individual person.

A verbal problem contributed to the discussion about the encyclical. Many translations of the encyclical actually employed the word socialization, whereas the original Latin phrase was *socialium rationum incrementa* (par. 59), which is translated as the multiplication of social relationships. However, the reality of the call for greater government intervention is not dependent only on the word socialization.[18] Commentators on the papal teaching also pointed out the significance of this new development in papal social teaching emphasizing a greater need for state intervention than heretofore precisely because of the development and complexities of existing problems. J.Y. Calvez insisted on the importance of socialization in the thought of Pope John but also tried to show that there had been a growing development in this direction. Pope Pius XII previously pointed out both a correct and an erroneous use of the term socialization.[19] An article in the semiauthoritative *Civiltà Cattolica* on the function of the state in light of the principle of subsidiarity and of the teaching of *Mater et magistra* recognized the need for a more vast, necessary, and fruitful intervention of the state to overcome existing imbalances, both in industry and in agriculture. The author sees the encyclical as inviting Catholics to a new era and a new epoch of social solidarity.[20]

In 1963 Pope John XXIII in the encyclical *Pacem in terris* continued to develop the same basic approach. Civil authorities should make earnest efforts to bring about situations in which individual citizens can easily exercise their rights and fulfill their duties. The state must give attention to the social as well as the economic progress of its citizens and to the development of such essential services as transportation, communications, water supply, housing, public health, and insurance systems, so that in the case of misfortune or increased family responsibilities no person will be without the necessary means to maintain a decent standard of living.[21] *Pacem in terris* begins with an insistence on the universal, inviolable, and inalienable rights of the human being as a person. The first right is to life, bodily integrity, and the means necessary for one's proper development. "Therefore, a human being also has the right to security in cases of sickness, inability to work, widowhood, old age, unemployment or in any other case in which he is deprived of the means of subsistence through no fault of his own."[22] Subsequent papal teaching has continued this emphasis on an enlarged scope for state activity, with the purpose of promoting and not suffocating the rights of individuals.

In addition to insisting on the rights of individuals contemporary Catholic social teaching continues to emphasize the importance and rights of the family as the foundation of society. Public authority has the duty to recognize, protect, and promote the true nature and rights of the family.[23] In the fall of 1983 the Vatican issued "A Charter of the Rights of the Family," which briefly touches on some of the issues under consideration in this paper. Families have the right to measures in the social domain which take into account their needs, especially in the event of difficult circumstances involving extra burdens put on the family by the old age of one of its members. The elderly have the right to find in their own family or, if this is not possible, in suitable institutions an environment conducive to their well-being and security.[24]

A proper understanding of the Catholic tradition on the role of the state today cannot merely quote Pius XI and argue against state involvement.[25] In this context it is necessary to note that here in the United States there was at the time of John XXIII and is today much less government involvement than in most European states. However, even in a worldwide perspective Pope John XXIII was pointing out the need for a greater state involvement than heretofore. The contemporary reality of increased social relationships calls for a larger role for the state in its efforts to promote fundamental human rights and the rights of the family than was true at the time of Pope Pius XI in 1931.

Official Catholic social teaching thus insists on the rights of the aged. Rights language is the strongest moral language and involves much more than just ideals or values. A right can be described as that which is due someone as one's own. There are four essential aspects of any right — the subject of the right, or the person involved; the object, or the matter of the right; the title, which is the fact by reason of which one claims the right; and the term, which refers to the person or group affected by a right and having the corresponding duty.

In applying the Catholic teaching to the aged the subject of the right is the aged person. The object of the right is the social security and health necessary and suitable for that person for the proper development of one's life in accord with one's capabilities. The title in this case is the very fact of old age with the needs and insecurities which may accompany it. Many individuals and others have some responsibility for the aged. The ultimate term of the right, or the one with the final obligation to see that the right if fulfilled, is society in general which works through the political arm of the state. The state can call upon individuals themselves, families, and others to fulfill the obligation resulting from the rights of the aged, or the state itself can provide what is needed.

How are we to understand the obligation and the duty of the state? The relationship existing between individuals and between individuals and society are governed by the virtue of justice. It will be helpful to recall briefly the meaning of justice developed in the last chapter. There are three different types of justice in the traditional Catholic approach. Commutative justice regulates the relationships existing between one individual and another. Distributive justice governs the relationship between the social whole or the state and the individual members of society. Legal justice orders the relationship of individuals to the social whole or the state.

In the case of society's relationship to the aged distributive justice is involved. There is a very important difference between commutative justice and distributive justice. Commutative justice involves arithmetic equality and is totally blind to the nature and condition of the persons involved. Distributive justice concerns the proper distribution of the goods and burdens of society to the different members. The equality involved here is proportional, which by its very nature must be related to the person or persons involved as distinct from an arithmetic equality which deals only with the thing itself and abstracts from the person. The subjective aspect to distributive justice is evident in the sense that the person must be taken into account. Civil authorities, for example, with the power to make appointments to various offices should appoint only those who are qualified. The qualifications of the person must be taken into account.

Different types of goods are to be distributed in society. Basic human rights such as the right to life and the right to freedom are based on the dignity of the human person and

belong to all. The present discussion refers to what have traditionally been called external goods, such as food, clothing,
shelter, education, and such. In the case of external goods
the Catholic tradition insists that everyone has the right to
those goods which are necessary for living a minimally decent human existence. Society and the state have the obligation to distribute external goods in this way, which is not a
full picture of distributive justice but describes the basic floor
or minimum to which all have a right. In the distribution of
these external goods society or the state must not be blind
but must respond to the needs of people. The state's obligation of distributive justice corresponds to the basic right of
the individual to have what is necessary for a minimally descent human existence.

This understanding of the rights of the person and the corresponding obligations of the state in distributive justice to
make sure that the basic needs of its citizens are met corresponds with the understanding of the purpose of the goods
of creation. Official Catholic teaching in the last few decades
has emphasized what the heart of the tradition has always
highlighted — the fact that the goods of creation exist to serve
the needs of all. Pope Paul VI, in the light of the universal
destiny of the goods of creation to serve the needs of all, insists in his 1967 encyclical *Populorum progressio*, "All other rights
whatsoever, including those of property and free commerce,
are to be subordinated to this principle." Thus private property does not constitute for anyone an absolute and uncondi-
tional right.[26] The most recent Catholic teaching emphasizes
the preferential option for the poor.[27] This general emphasis
would certainly support and even strengthen the obligation
of the state to make sure that the elderly have what is necessary
for decent human existence, including their participation in
civil and social existence to the extent possible.

The state thus has the ultimate obligation to insure that
the aged have what is necessary for a basically decent human
existence. But how should the state carry out this function?
It is the contention here that the state should not require filial
fiscal help for an aged parent in need. Many reasons support
such a contention.

First, the historical development of policy in the United States has emphasized a greater role of the state in caring for the elderly and at least until 1983 the total elimination of legally enforceable filial fiscal contributions to aged parents in need.[28] In the United States since 1935 various programs have been developed to provide for the elderly. The social security program consists in a universal, compulsory, contributory, social insurance program for one's retirement and old age. Contributions are made by the employer and the individual person as the employee. The Supplemental Security Income program (SSI) guarantees that the annual income of an older or disabled person will not fall below a minimum floor. In addition, Medicare since 1966 provides hospital insurance and a supplemental medical insurance program for the aged. Medicare programs were designed to help the aged pay for medical care. In addition to these age entitlement programs are needed entitlement programs that often affect the elderly but are not directed only to the elderly. Most significant for the elderly are Medicaid, which finances medical services for public assistance recipients and those deemed medically indigent; housing subsidies of different kinds; food stamps, which have been described as a negative income tax earmarked for food. Notice how the state has become gradually more involved, but that the individual and the employer are also part of the total program. Also, the individual through private pension plans or with one's employer is able to provide more retirement income, possibilities which appeal especially to the middle- and upper-income brackets. Until 1983 no legal way was adopted to require any filial financial responsibility for the needs of the aged who are not able to take care of themselves. The practice in this country has developed much more slowly than in most Western industrialized nations, but the pattern is the same in terms of no requirements of a legally enforced fiscal responsibility for an aged poor parent. The development of the present policy over the last few decades in the United States appears to be an illustration of the development of the role of the state and of the principle of subsidiarity in Catholic teaching. In the midst of the growing socialization and complexity of human existence the state today must take over some of the role that had previously been fulfilled by families and voluntary associations in society.

Second, even those who might disagree with the general development in the last decades recognize that practically it would be most difficult, if not impossible, to go back to a policy of compulsory filial fiscal responsibility for the needy elderly. For practical reasons it is very difficult to bring about changes of this type. This conclusion logically leads into and depends somewhat upon the next consideration.

Third, the changing financial and sociological situation of the elderly argues against legally enforced filial fiscal responsibility. The historical development of the past fifty years in this country has had the effect of enabling and enhancing the independence of the elderly. Programs have created a climate stressing such independence. Financial independence has led to the possibility of independence in other areas, especially in terms of housing and residence. Families have been relieved of the burden of providing for and caring for an aged parent in ordinary circumstances. It is true that at some time some aged might well become dependent on others again. However, at the end of many years of such independence to enforce legally the need for adult children to be financially responsible for an aged parent in need would be difficult.

Fourth, from the perspective of the family, to accept such a legal obligation to support an elderly parent would be burdensome. The nuclear family has concentrated on parental responsibility for one's own children. Parents provide for the necessary cost of raising and educating their own children. In addition, parents have an obligation to prepare for their own retirement and old age. Thus, prior obligations take precedence before one can speak of an adult child's financial obligation to one's own aged parent. Surveys of public opinion indicate that most of the elderly and of adult children agree that adult children do not have a financial responsibility for their aged parents. Especially when questions are framed in the light of a context such as other responsibilities to one's children or to oneself, only a minority of the aged (5-15 percent) affirm the responsibility of adult children to support their aged parents.[29] The manifold obligations existing within the nuclear family today make it very difficult to assert an absolute moral obligation to provide financially for aged parents which should legally be enforced.

Fifth, contemporary developments in the family also militate against the existence of such an obligation in the legal area. The elderly parent has usually not been a part of the family household with the adult child. Today the four-generation family is coming to be the norm. This reality further complicates the picture because of the obligations which now might flow over a number of generations. In the contemporary scene the fact of divorce also brings a new element into the picture. Often an adult child might not feel close to a natural parent because the child was not raised by that parent. The complexities of family existence today add further reason for not asserting a legally enforceable filial responsibility to care for an aged parent.

Sixth, the problem also arises of legally enforcing an obligation which is so difficult to plan and prepare for. As mentioned, the now adult children have many other obligations. Presumably the aged parent has made some financial preparations for old age when possible. Whether or not any other money will be needed depends on circumstances beyond anyone's control. It is problematic to plan in the midst of such uncertainty. Perhaps nothing will be needed; perhaps because of chronic illness a great deal of financial help will be necessary. Since it is so difficult for an adult child to prepare for this eventuality facing an older parent and since one must plan for one's own older age and other obligations, it is not appropriate to enforce legally such an obligation on adult children.

Seventh, the very nature of the problem also leads to the conclusion that the state should make provision for it. Not all people are going to require expensive assistance in their old age. Some will and many will not. Generally speaking the individual has little or no control over whether one will need such care. The severe infirmities associated with old age have a random character about them and lie beyond the range of personal responsibility for contracting them. That a society as a whole make provision for people who need such care is fitting in the same way that society makes provision for the unemployed and the disabled.

Eighth, practical problems are connected with enforcing such payments. In a number of cases no real bond of human relationship seems to exist between the aged person and an adult child. Sometimes contact has been lost for years. These circumstances make enforceability more difficult. In addition the costs of enforceability would be comparatively high and not proportionate to the money that would be recovered for the public treasury. The practical problems are even more complex when the individuals involved live in different state jurisdictions. These practical considerations weighed heavily in the decisions not to demand such compulsory contributions by adult children to the Medicaid and Supplemental Security Income programs. Thus a number of different reasons argue for the state to provide for the elderly in need and not to require by law that adult children support such an elderly parent.

III. The Moral Obligations of Adult Children to an Elderly Parent

The last section has made the point that recent historical developments, a contemporary understanding of the role of families and of the state, the very nature of the obligation, and difficulties in enforcement argue against a legal requirement for adult children to provide financial assistance for aged parents in need. However, a moral obligation in general does exist for adult children to care for an aged parent. This general moral obligation is grounded in the very nature of the parent-child relationship and in what the parent has previously done for the child. The primary general responsibility of adult children to aged parents is one of care, concern, and personal relationships. Aging parents have generally been quite independent of their children as the children themselves have matured and lived out their own responsibilities, but the parental relationship with adult children should have continued over these years. In reality, many adult children seem to have such good relationships with an aged parent, even though in fact estrangements in relationships are often present between elderly parents and their adult children. The obligations of care, concern, and general relationship correspond to what family members can most appropriately give to one another. Emphasis in the last decade on the role of grandparents has helped to solidify and strengthen relationships between adult children and aged parents. In most circumstances adult children can be one of the significant relationships in the life of an aged parent, but not necessarily the most significant or the most important.

Two difficult moral dilemmas concern the responsibility of adult children to support financially an aged parent in need and the obligation to bring a functionally dependent adult parent into one's own home. The question of financial help is somewhat less complicated. In this case a moral obligation to help an aged parent undoubtedly exists if this can be done without disproportionate harm to one's obligation to one's own spouse, children and self. The general principle is quite clear, but in practice difficult prudential moral decisions must be made.

The question of bringing a functionally dependent aged parent into the home of an adult child, especially if this is the only way to avoid institutionalization, presents even more complexity. The question of financial help involves only the monetary question. However, human relationships of the aged parent with the existing family of the adult child as well as the capabilities of such a family in caring for the aged parent are important factors that also must be considered in the second case. Now and even more so in the future often no one will be at home to care for the aged parent since both spouses are often working, and none of their children are at home.

At times an adult child might be willing to bring an aged parent into one's home but is unable to do so without added help. Living with an adult child or some other person is much more appropriate for an aged parent than unnecessary institutionalization. However, at times institutionalization is both appropriate and necessary. If an elderly parent can appropriately live with an adult child, it is less costly and eases the financial burden of the state in the case of the elderly who are poor and in need. Both in general and in the specific case of the needy the state should help to maintain the functionally dependent elderly in an appropriate home situation so that unnecessary institutionalization can be avoided. The role of the state in these circumstances is a good illustration of the principle of subsidiarity at work.

Unfortunately, at the present time supplemental security income is reduced by one-third if one receives support and maintenance by living in another person's household. This provision directly affects the poor and dependent elderly living with their families or others. The government should try to encourage such living together, and therefore many have rightly recommended that the reduction in supplemental security income be dropped for the elderly living in another household.[30] To encourage adult children and others who are willing to provide for a functionally dependent aged person in their own homes, the government should provide some help. Most elderly people do not want to be institutionalized, nor do adult children want a functionally dependent aged parent to be institutionalized if this can be avoided. Despite all the provisions made to encourage institutionalization at least on the part of the providers, the percentage of the aged institutionalized in the United States has not grown. Many proposals have been made for the state to make provisions enabling adult children to care for a functionally dependent parent in one's own home. The provision of such services in a direct manner has been proposed. Others call for an attendance allowance which is already provided in many countries with the option left to the beneficiary whether help at home is purchased, provided by the family, or not provided at all. Others support a greater social security benefit for the old-old as a way of dealing with the same problem.[31] In summary, help can and should be provided to encourage adult children to care for a functionally dependent parent at home if this is feasible. Such an approach seems to be good practical application of the principle of subsidiarity.

IV. A Final Conclusion

This chapter has considered the filial responsibility to an aged parent and argued against a legally enforced financial contribution. However, it is necessary to view this particular problem within a wider context in order to at least recognize all the dimensions involved. A broader theoretical question or problem has often been brought up as an objection against Catholic social teaching. According to this objection too much emphasis is given in the Catholic teaching to distribution and not enough to production.[32] This general objection when applied to the particular case under consideration involves the acute problem of how government is going to pay for these programs for the aged. Catholic theology insists on a just distribution. All have a right to a basically decent human existence, and government has a special obligation to provide for the aged and the disabled. But one must address the question of providing the money for such a role.

A broader practical problem is also somewhat connected with the theoretical question mentioned above. The aged in our society still need help. In 1982 one out of seven aged were poor by the government's own definition of what constitutes the poverty line.[33] Probably many other aged belong to the invisible poor. The aged poor also have many other needs which are not being met. Medicare was created to meet the needs of the aged in paying for acute medical care. However, the health problems of the aged are often chronic, and such cases are not really covered under Medicare. In addition the needs of the aged involve not only health but also social services such as transportation, personal care, homemaker assistance, and meal preparation. These needs very often are not being met.

At the same time the existing programs, which in the light of the above are inadequate, are themselves costing more money than is available. There has been a growing debate about and actual changes made in the social security program to assure its fiscal integrity in the future. Also much discussion has taken place about the growing cost of Medicare and the need for cost containment in the light of escalating medical costs.

My own position based on the Catholic tradition argues that more should be done for the elderly and that the state must assume much of the burden. However, this only increases the dilemma about how to pay for such services. One comparatively short paper cannot possibly be expected even to attempt to solve this question, but on the other hand one would be irresponsible not to address the problem. One cannot call for state involvement and even greater state financial involvement without addressing the issue of cost and the provision of resources.

In this connection distributive justice with its emphasis on proportional equality also applies to how the tax burden is to be distributed. The last chapter has developed the rationale for a progressive tax structure. Unfortunately the American tax structure is much less progressive today than it was a few decades ago. Taxes may have to be raised, but the tax burden must fall more heavily on the rich.

Concerning social security ways are available in which the cost of the system can be somewhat lessened. Government itself can make some contribution toward the system as is done in many industrialized countries of the West. More help must be given to the poor among the elderly, but money could be saved by doing away with the double tax exemption now granted the elderly. Also, three-quarters of the social security benefits received could be taxed, thereby providing more revenue for the system. Such changes in taxation would not be harmful to the poor. Efforts could also be made to push back the time of retirement in the future and thereby save money for the system.[34]

The Medicare system is presently experiencing difficulties in cost containment. And serious problems with Medicare are evident. The system as it exists does not really address the real challenge, does nothing to change the system of health-care delivery in the United States, and has been a positive factor in the escalation of health-care costs in this country. The Medicare system was designed to give the elderly the means to pay for acute medical care. However, the elderly also need chronic medical care and social services. In the light of existing political pressure Medicare has done nothing to change the health-care delivery system but has only encouraged the present system of fee for services in the development of evermore expensive and technologically sophisticated institutions as the centers for health care.[35] Our health-care system is in need of radical change. Such change can contribute to controlling the costs of health care. Ways of providing the money to meet the needs of a proper care for the aged in our society can be found.

In conclusion, this study has considered the moral obligations of adult children to elderly parents but argued against a legally enforced filial responsibility for an aged parent. In accord with a contemporary understanding of the principle of subsidiarity the state has a large role to play in care for the aged, especially those in need and in poverty. Difficult decisions are to be made about costs and raising revenue, but the state has the obligation to make sure that the aged have what is necessary for a basically decent life in the light of their human dignity and personhood.

NOTES

1. Cited in Odin W. Anderson, "Reflections on the Sick Aged and the Helping Systems," in Bernice L. Neugarten and Robert J. Havighurst, eds., *Social Policy, Social Ethics, and the Aging Society* (Washington, DC: National Science Foundation, U.S. Government Printing Office, 1976), pp. 89-96.

2. Brian Tierney, *Medieval Poor Law: A Sketch of Canonical Theory and Its Application in England* (Berkeley: University of California Press, 1959).

3. Ibid., p. 109.

4. Alvin Schorr, " . . . *Thy Father and Thy Mother . . .": A Second Look at Filial Responsibility and Family Policy* (Washington, DC: U.S. Department of Health and Human Services, Social Security Administation, 1980), pp. 8,9.

5. For different essays on this historical development see Ethel Shanas and Marvin B. Sussman, eds., *Family, Bureaucracy, and the Elderly* (Durham, NC: Duke University Press, 1977), pp. 36-171.

6. Robert J. Buchanan, "Medicaid: Family Responsibility and Long-Term Care," *The Journal of Long-Term Care Administration* 12 (Fall 1984): 19.

7. Ibid., pp. 24, 25.

8. U.S. Senate Special Committe on Aging in Conjunction with the American Association of Retired Persons, *Aging America: Trends and Projections* (Washington, DC, 1984), p. 86.

9. Schorr, ". . . *Thy Father and Thy Mother . . .*," pp. 13-32.

10. Ibid., p. 12.

11. For the development of the different roles and functions in the life of society according to the Catholic tradition see Jacques Maritain, *Man and the State* (Chicago: University of Chicago Press Phoenix Books, 1956); Johannes Messner, *Social Ethics: Natural Law in the Western World* (St. Louis: B. Herder, 1965); Heinrich A. Rommen, *The State in Catholic Thought: A Treatise in Political Philosophy* (St. Louis: B. Herder, 1950).

12. Helmut Thielicke, *Theological Ethics*, vol. 2: *Politics* (Philadelphia: Fortress Press, 1969).

13. David Hollenbach, *Claims in Conflict: Retrieving and Renewing the Catholic Human Rights Tradition* (New York: Paulist, 1979).

14. Pope Pius XI, *Quadragesimo anno*, par. 79, 80, in Terence P. McLaughlin, ed., *The Church and the Reconstruction of the Modern World: The Social Encyclicals of Pope Pius XI* (Garden City, NY: Doubleday Image Books, 1957), pp. 246, 247.

15. For arguments against a restrictive interpretation of the principle of subsidiarity proposed at that time see Benjamin L. Masse, *Justice for All: An Introduction to the Social Teaching of the Catholic Church* (Milwaukee: Bruce, 1964), pp. 75ff.

16. Pope John XXIII, *Mater et magistra*, in Joseph Gremillion, ed., *The Gospel of Peace and Justice* (Maryknoll, NY: Orbis, 1976), pp. 143-200.

17. Gary Wills, *Politics and Catholic Freedom* (Chicago: Henry Regnery, 1964); "This Week," *National Review* 11 (July 29, 1961): 38; "For the Record," *National Review* 11 (August 12, 1961): 77.

18. Edmond Dougan, "Socialization: The Principles," *Christus Rex* 17 (1963): 136-150.

19. Jean Yves Calvez, "La socialisation dans la pensée de l'église," *Revue de L'Action Populaire* 158 (1962): 517-522.

20. Guiseppe M. Diez-Alegria, "La funzione dello stato nell'economia politica secondo il principio di sussidarietà," *La Civiltà Cattolica* 113, n. 3 (1962): 417-430.

21. Pope John XXIII, *Pacem in terris*, par. 63, 64, in Gremillion, *The Gospel of Peace and Justice*, p. 215.

22. Pope John XXIII, *Pacem in terris*, par. 9-11, in ibid., p. 203.

23. Gremillion, *The Gospel of Peace and Justice*, pp. 111, 112.

24. Pontifical Council for the Family, "Charter of Rights of the Family," *Origins* 13 (December 15, 1983): 461-464.

25. For an example of such an approach, see Charles Dechert, "Subsidiarity and Voluntarism in Mass Society," *Social Thought* 6 (1980): 41-57.

26. Pope Paul VI, *Populorum progressio*, par. 22-24, in Gremillion, *The Gospel of Peace and Justice*, p. 394.

27. Donal Dorr, *Option for the Poor: A Hundred years of Vatican Social Teaching* (Maryknoll, NY: Orbis, 1983).

28. Shanas and Sussman, *Family, Bureaucracy, and the Elderly*, pp. 36-171; Bryan Gold, Elizabeth Kutza, and Theodore R. Mamor, "United States Social Policy on Old Age: Present Patterns and Predictions," in Neugarten and Havighurst, *Social Policy*, pp. 9-22.

29. Schorr, ". . . . *Thy Father and Thy Mother* . . .," p. 12.

30. Ibid., pp. 28-30.

31. Ibid., pp. 32-39.

32. Michael Novak, *The Spirit of Democratic Capitalism* (New York: Simon and Schuster, 1982), p. 24.

33. *Aging America*, p. 36.

34. Robert M. Ball, "Income Security after Retirement," in Neugarten and Havighurst, *Social Policy*, pp. 33-44; Ball, "Social Security: Today and Tomorrow" (New York: Columbia University Press, 1978).

35. Henry P. Brehm and Rodney M. Coe, *Health Care for the Aged: From Social Problem to Federal Program* (New York: Praeger, 1980).

7: Religious Freedom and Human Rights in the World and in the Church: A Christian Perspective

Human rights and religious liberty are receiving worldwide attention in the last few years. In the past and even in the present many violations of human rights have occurred in the name of religious belief. The source of the problem is evident. Most religions involve a belief in a divine power and gift which brings life, salvation, and liberation to human beings. This belief is certainly true of Christianity, which professes Jesus as the Savior of the world. A conviction that belief in Jesus and in a particular Christian denomination is so important has been used for centuries to override the religious freedom and human rights of other people. There are many situations in the modern world in which religions do not grant religious liberty or toleration to others and in the process deny basic human rights. Think of the religious struggles in Iran, in the Near East, in Northern Ireland, in Bangladesh, in India, and in so many other parts of the world.

Always a tension exists between a passionate religious belief in salvation through one particular way and the toleration of others or an acceptance of their religious liberty. For the nonbeliever or even for one who maintains that all religions are basically the same, very little tension is present between saving religious truth and the freedom of those who do not so believe. Even today problems emerge more often among religious fanatics and fundamentalists. Mainstream Western Christianity has taken a long time to work out a way of respecting human rights and liberty while holding on to the truth-claims of Christianity.

Despite widespread practical violations of human rights and

religious liberty in our modern world because of religion, great progress has been made in the world community due to a theoretical recognition of the importance and meaning of religious liberty and human rights. The most significant embodiment of this important worldwide development is found in the declarations, conventions, and work of the United Nations. The Universal Declaration of Human Rights was adopted in December 1948. This basic document has been developed over the years by subsequent statements, declarations, and conventions. In 1983 the United Nations published a 146-page compendium of international instruments of human rights.[1] The occasion was the celebration of the thirty-fifth anniversary of the adoption of the Universal Declaration of Human Rights. After a long and tortuous development the Declaration on the Elimination of All Forms of Intolerance and of Discrimination Based on Religion or Belief was adopted without a vote by the General Assembly of the United Nations on November 25, 1981. Many aspects of these documents can and should be criticized, but they nevertheless represent a great achievement and advancement for humankind. Despite cultural, religious, linguistic, economic, political, and ideological differences, these documents point to a general consensus in the world community, at least in theory, on the matter of human rights in general and religious liberty in particular.

Mainline Protestant and Roman Catholic churches have also come to general agreement on the matter of human rights and religious liberty, or tolerence, which is not exactly the same as religious liberty.[2] Protestant Christianity was first to accept religious liberty, which only became a part of official Catholic teaching at the Second Vatican Council in 1965.[3] Mainstream Western Christianity is in basic agreement about the meaning of religious liberty. The right to religious liberty is not only the freedom to have a certain belief, but also involves the freedom of religious expression, the freedom of religious association, and corporate and institutional religious freedom.[4]

Western Christianity has recently embraced the concept of human rights as exemplified in official statements by the Roman Catholic Church, the Word Council of Churches, the Lutheran World Federation, and the World Alliance of

Reformed Churches.[5] Human rights is a very complex issue, but official statements and theological writings have rightly recognized and even endorsed this complexity. At the first level human rights are seen primarily as political and civil rights defending the freedom of individuals against the power of the state. In distinction from this approach of Western democracies socialist nations have insisted on social and economic rights. Third World considerations have developed the concept of rights even further, and recent rights discussions have recognized rights to development, to a good environment, and to peace. In general Catholic and Protestant statements and theologians insist on the broad approach to human rights. There are different understandings of the grounding of human rights and religious liberty, but remarkable agreement among mainline Protestants and Catholics exists on the meaning, nature, and extension of these rights.

Western Christianity, however, has taken a long time and a difficult path to arrive at its acceptance of religious liberty and fundamental human rights. Christians can only rejoice at what has occurred, but aspects of the question continue to be of importance both for society at large and the church. The first aspect concerns how the mainline Protestant and Catholic churches came to the acceptance of these rights. This question has not only historical and theoretical significance but also practical bearing. Perhaps history can help to show how other religions and the world itself can come to the same acceptance of human rights. The second aspect of the question concerns the recognition of freedom and human rights within the churches themselves. How in theory and in practice do the churches themselves recognize and safeguard the religious freedom and rights of their own members? These two aspects will be developed in the two major sections of this paper.

I. An Analysis of the Past

In general Roman Catholic and mainline Protestant Christianity contributed little or nothing to the original acceptance of religious liberty in the West. The Christian churches and Christian theology arrived on the scene both late and breathless. Church and theological support for religious liberty came only after religious liberty had already been well accepted in the West. Protestantism in general embraced religious liberty much earlier than Roman Catholicism. American Protestantism accepted religious liberty before European mainline Protestantism, but recall that religious establishment continued to exist in Massachusetts until 1833.[6] However, even in the 1960s prominent Protestant scholars such as Thomas Sanders and Philip Wogaman pointed out that while American Protestantism had for a long time supported religious freedom, no common theological understanding and grounding of the principle of religious liberty was endorsed.[7]

Two factors seemed to play a very important role in the acceptance of religious liberty in Western civilization from the seventeenth century on. These two factors are the secularization of the state and the recognition of the existence of religious pluralism. The secularization of the state and the breakdown of the old Christendom model put into historical actuality the dualism between church and state. Without doubt in many countries the secularization of the state was based on some antichurch and antireligious motives which made it all the harder for some religionists to accept the religious liberty proposed by such advocates. The existence of religious pluralism was also a very pragmatic reason for accepting religious freedom. Religious freedom was the only practical solution in the midst of a religious pluralism that was above all exemplified in the United States.

The historical circumstances affected the approach of the Christian churches to religious liberty. No doctrine of religious liberty was present in the Reformation, and the seventeenth-century solution *cuius regio eius religio* — the religion of the people follows the religion of the prince — was the recognized approach of mainstream Protestantism. Later, however, not only the Protestant sects but also the mainline Protestant churches often found themselves as a minority religion striving for their own existence and survival. Religious liberty was intimately connected with their continued existence and development. Even when some churches gained religious liberty for themselves, as in England for example, they saw no need to extend it to others, such as Jews and Catholics.

The Roman Catholic Church only endorsed religious liberty fully in the 1960s. Before that time the famous distinction between thesis and hypothesis appeared to many as sheer opportunism. That Catholic distinction exhibited a willingness to tolerate religious liberty in those situations in which religious pluralism existed, but it maintained that the ideal is the denial of religious liberty and the union of all in the one, true Catholic faith. In practice, where Catholics were the overwhelming majority, religious liberty was denied; but where Catholics were a minority, religious liberty was accepted. Thus, historical factors brought about the acceptance of religious liberty in the West, and its later acceptance by the churches was heavily motivated by self-interest and institutional concerns.

Although the emergence of religious liberty in the West was not originally due to church policies or theology and although practical reasons of institutional self-interest were of great importance in the churches' acceptance of religious liberty, theological resources within the two major Christian traditions in the West could be used to justify and support religious freedom. In the course of time both Protestants and finally Roman Catholics have found this support in their own traditions.

Protestant Justification of Religious Freedom

The fact that Protestantism embraced religious freedom before Catholicism is not due only to more pragmatic reasons, for in general Protestantism has always given more importance to freedom than has Catholicism. Specifically from the perspectives of theology, epistemology, ethics, political ethics, and ecclesiology, Protestantism has given a more central role to freedom than has Roman Catholicism. From a theological perspective, Protestantism has emphasized salvation by faith which frees Christians from the law. Freedom is the description often given to the redeemed status of the believer through the gracious gift of God in Christ Jesus. However, some classical Protestants so stressed divine predestination that they downplayed human freedom. Roman Catholicism has always insisted on both faith and works and has not been accustomed to speaking about the redeemed state of the believer primarily in terms of freedom. The very ethos of much Protestant thought has accentuated freedom. The basic thrust of Protestantism was a reaction against the authoritarianism of the Church of Rome. The Protestant Reform often appealed to freedom and gave it an important role in its self-understanding.

Epistemologically, Roman Catholicism has insisted that the word and work of God are mediated in and through reason and human nature. Reason and reason's ability to know the truth have been stressed in Catholicism. Orthodoxy has always been a very central consideration, as well as the church's ability to know with certitude and to communicate the truths of faith. Such an approach leaves little room for tolerance and freedom with regard to religious truth. This emphasis on the ability of human beings to reason and to know the truth with certitude has not been as central in Protestantism. In more recent times Paul Tillich developed what he called the Protestant principle—which is basically the protest against any absolute claims made for finite and relative reality.[8] Our knowledge of God is never perfect but always inadequate and always under the judgment of the absolute. The Protestant principle is much broader than the question of truth, but it is applicable here. In the light of such a principle the Protestant approach could never be as totally self-confident of the truth as the Catholic position. Philip Wogaman has invoked this Protestant principle to criticize all absolute claims on the basis of which religious liberty could be denied.[9] Contemporary Catholic thought, however, with its more eschatological emphasis, often finds itself quite sympathetic to Tillich's Protestant principle.

Protestant ethics, although not as developed as Catholic ethics, has given great centrality to freedom.[10] Perhaps it is this very emphasis on freedom which has contributed to the fact that Protestant ethics has not been developed as systematically as Catholic ethics. God in Protestant ethics is often understood in terms of freedom. God freely chooses to make a covenant with human beings and to redeem the human race. God is ever and always free to intervene in history, for God is the sovereign of history. Catholic ethics puts less stress on freedom both in God and in human beings. God acts in accord with the divine plan. The natural law is nothing more than the participation in the rational creature of the eternal law. Human reason reflecting on human nature can arrive at the divine plan for the world. James Gustafson has recently pointed out an interesting convergence which has occurred in the last few years in Christian ethics. Protestant ethics is searching for some structure to overcome the occasionalism and existentialism that came from too great an insistence on freedom, whereas Catholic ethics is striving to overcome the traditional emphasis on order and find room for responsible openness.[11] Historically and traditionally, however, Protestant ethics has stressed freedom, whereas Roman Catholic moral theology has insisted on order.

In social ethics much discussion has focused on the relationship of the different faiths to democratic government. Historically, Roman Catholicism opposed the early democratic revolutions and was not favorable to democracy. Until very recently Catholic thought was indifferent about forms of government and saw no great advantage in democracy.[12] Some affinity seems to have existed between later Calvinism and democracy, but again this depended somewhat on circumstances.[13] In Europe Calvinism was often associated with efforts to revolt from the absolute power of the ruler and therefore supported democratic forms of government, but a form of Calvinism continues to support the government of South Africa with its apartheid principles. Protestantism in the United States was a strong supporter of democracy. The traditional Protestant emphasis on sin has also played a role in Protestant acceptance of democracy by recognizing possible abuse of power and the need to protect people against such abuses. The division of powers among the executive, legislative, and judicial branches has often been defended in Protestantism on the basis of the need to protect against the abuses arising from sin. No one individual or group should be trusted with all the power. Reinhold Niebuhr has maintained that the capacity of human beings for justice makes democracy possible, but the inclination of human beings to injustice makes democracy necessary.[14] Even in social ethics Catholic thought until recently has not seen freedom as an important value. This aspect of Catholic social ethics will be developed later in greater detail.

The Protestant emphasis on freedom has also strongly affected Protestant ecclesiology and its difference from Catholic ecclesiology. From the very beginning Protestantism has insisted on the freedom of the believer. Catholic theology with its emphasis on the human has always taken mediation seriously. The word and work of God are mediated in and through the human. Thus the church as a human reality mediates the divine gift of salvation. The church community is a sign or sacrament that makes visible and present the mercy and presence of God in our world. In all of theology mediation has characterized the Catholic approach with its traditional inistence on the "and" — faith *and* reason, grace *and* nature, scripture *and* tradition, Jesus *and* the church, divine law *and* natural law. The abuse in the Catholic understanding is to absolutize what is only the mediation, and this has often happened in different areas, especially in ecclesiology. Thus, the role of the church has been absolutized, and for many people the church was supreme even over the scriptures themselves. Protestantism has stressed the immediate relationship of the believer with God and downplayed the role of the visible church. The church is not seen as mediating the word and work of Jesus to the believer through the visible community itself. The believer is in immediate contact with the word of God in the scripture. Catholic ecclesiology has tended to be more communitarian, whereas Protestantism has tended to be more individualistic. Not only has Catholicism insisted on the role of the church as a visible community, but the community is hierarchically structured with special powers of teaching, ruling, and sanctifying given to the offices of pope and bishop. In reaction to Protestantism post-Tridentine Catholicism tended to define itself not primarily as the people of God but as a hierarchically structured society. Most theologians agree that since the Reformation the Catholic

Church became overly authoritarian, and Vatican Council II tried to overcome some of the theoretical and practical abuses of authoritarianism.

Although Protestantism historically has been more open to and supportive of freedom in general than has Roman Catholicism, this emphasis is not without problems of its own, as hinted at in some of the above analysis, but it does explain why Protestantism could historically be more open to religious freedom than Catholicism. However, there is a central tenet of Christianity that both Protestants and Catholics have appealed to in their later acceptance of religious liberty: the act of faith must be a free, personal assent. God's whole way of acting with human beings is to call for a free response to God's gracious gift. Many defenses of religious liberty have appealed to this fundamental tenet of Christian faith, but obviously what is called the social aspect of religious liberty includes much more than just protecting the private conscience of the individual.

Roman Catholic Justification of Religious Freedom

The Roman Catholic rejection of religious liberty before the Second Vatican Council must be seen in the light of its opposition to what was called modern liberalism with its emphasis on liberty in all its forms. An overview of the historical development within Roman Catholicism will be helpful for this present study.[15] The heavy emphasis in Catholic thinking was on objective truth and the natural law. At best one had to freely accept truth in the speculative order and natural law in the moral order, but freedom was never an ultimate value. The most important realities were the objective realities themselves, and truth in both the speculative and the practical orders could be known without too much difficulty. This emphasis was the basis for the famous statement that error has no rights.

From such a philosophical perspective modern liberalism with its stress on freedom and human reason apart from God denied the natural law and the all-important human relationship to God. Human beings and not God became the center of the universe, and God's law was shunted aside. The political aspects of this liberalism, especially as seen in the French Revolution, were clearly opposed to the Catholic notion of Christendom. In addition much of this liberalism was perceived to be anti-Catholic. Such liberalism with its emphasis on freedom also favored an individualism that was opposed to the Catholic understanding of society as an organic community of people working together for the common good.

These perspectives make it somewhat easier to understand, but not completely justify, the opposition by the Catholic Church even in the nineteenth century to the modern freedoms. Pope Gregory XVI and Pope Pius IX condemned freedom of conscience and worship as a madness. Freedom of speech and freedom of the press were likewise condemned.[16] Their successor Pope Leo XIII continued this attack on the modern freedoms. Some problems were apparent with the understanding of freedom proposed by liberalism, but Catholic thought refused to even dialogue with it and rejected the modern freedoms often by tenaciously holding on to a past that could no longer be a viable option.

The Catholic Church, which was the great enemy of freedom in the nineteenth century, gradually came to champion freedom in the twentieth century. Many factors explain this change, but a very important aspect was the emergence of a new opponent. In the nineteenth century, individualistic liberalism with its emphasis on freedom was seen as the primary problem of the age. However, as the twentieth century progressed, a new problem appeared on the scene — totalitarianism. Catholic social ethics has always tried to find a middle path between individualism and collectivisim. Against the collectivism of Fascism, Nazism, and Communism (but with much greater fear of the left) Catholic teaching defended the dignity and rights of the human person. Human freedom became very significant. The development came to its climax in the 1960s. One can see a very significant change even within the writings of Pope John XXIII. In 1961 in the encyclical *Mater et magistra* Pope John insisted that the ideal social order should be based on truth, justice, and love.[17] In *Pacem in terris*, issued two years later, John added a signifi-

cant element to this trilogy—truth, justice, love, and freedom.[18] With this official Catholic acceptance of the importance of human freedom in society, the one remaining obstacle
was the Catholic teaching on religious freedom, which was
changed by the Decree on Religious Freedom of the Second
Vatican Council in 1965.

The acceptance of religious liberty in the council was based
on the dignity of the human person. However, there was and
still is some dispute about the exact grounding or basis of the
right to religious liberty. John Courtney Murray, the American Jesuit whose influence on the Vatican II document was
greater than any other person, based religious liberty on
an understanding of limited constitutional government. For
Murray religious liberty was primarily a juridical and constitutional question with theological and ethical overtones. For
a number of French bishops and theologians religious liberty
was primarily a theological issue which should be addressed
from a specific theological perspective.[19] This discussion has
important ramifications for our understanding of freedom and
human rights in the church. By basing religious freedom on
the nature of constitutional government Murray's approach
could be interpreted to separate and distinguish too much between freedom within society and freedom within the church.
A more theological basis for religious freedom in civil society
would also furnish a more direct reason for affirming a greater
role for freedom within the church.[20]

The analysis thus far has been related only to freedom and
religious freedom, emphasizing how these realities came about
in the Western world without a major contribution from the
Christian churches or theologies. Subsequently, with no small
help from self-interest the churches have given a theological
basis and justification for religious liberty.

Western Christianity and Human Rights

What has been the general attitude of Western Christian
churches to the other part of our consideration—human rights?
Today the Protestant and Catholic churches are strong supporters of human rights understood in a rather complex way

and including more than the traditional rights of Western liber-
ties.[21] Very often today human rights language becomes one
way of talking about the whole of social ethics. To discuss
the whole history of Christian social ethics is impossible, but
a brief comment will indicate how Catholic and Protestant
churches and theologies have come to accept human-rights
terminology and understanding. In both traditions are strong
strains of justice and social concern, but only recently have
both churches come to accept and even endorse the terminology of human rights.

Human-rights language is not congenial to the Protestant
tradition with its emphasis on the primacy of God and God's
gracious gift of salvation.[22] To speak of human rights seems
to start in the wrong place and makes the human being the
center of all things. However, contemporary Protestant theologians have been able to accept the language of human rights
and integrate it into a broader theological perspective. Thus
the covenant and divine claims have been the grounding for
human rights in some contemporary Protestant theologians.[23]

The language and the universality of human rights follows
quite easily from a natural law approach, but Protestantism
has generally rejected such an approach and insisted on
something distinctively Christian. However, on the basis of
creation and covenant Protestant ethics has been able to support the universality of human rights for all. In practice contemporary Protestantism, especially through the work of the
World Council of Churches, has encouraged interest in and
participation by the younger churches of the Third World.
As a result the human rights concerns of the Third World
have been incorporated into the contemporary understanding
of human rights in mainstream Protestanism.

The natural law tradition associated with Roman Catholicism would seem in theory to be quite congenial with universal
rights ontologically grounded in the human person. However,
the Catholic tradition was slow to embrace the terminology
of human rights. The first full systematic development of
human rights in official Catholic teaching appeared in Pope
John XXIII's encyclical *Pacem in terris* in 1963. Catholic teaching and theology were not at home with the language of human

rights because the secular tradition supporting the "rights of man" was associated with an individualistic liberalism that was strongly opposed by Catholicism in the eighteenth and nineteenth centuries. Even the language of rights indicated a human autonomy cut off from God and God's law. The Catholic teaching insisted on following the natural law and not the rights of individuals. However, as the twentieth century progressed, the Catholic Church began to defend and stress the dignity of the human person and the rights of the individual. One advantage of its earlier opposition to individualistic rights was the recognition of social and economic rights when it finally adopted the human rights approach in *Pacem in terris*.

Contemporary Catholic social teaching continues its emphasis on human dignity and rights by calling attention to two significant human aspirations in the contemporary world — the aspiration to equality and the aspiration to participation, two forms of human dignity and freedom.[24] An older Catholic ethics was fearful of equality as destroying the organic nature of society in which the differentiated parts are organized in a hierarchical manner to achieve the common good. But now equality is no longer seen as detrimental to communal human existence. An older approach understood society as being structured from the top down, with the people at times even described as the ignorant masses who had to be directed by those in authority. Participation now stresses the right and need of all to share in creatively bringing about a more just social order for themselves and others. Thus the acceptance of and the importance of freedom, human rights, equality, and participation all point to a shift in Catholic thinking to a greater emphasis on the person and the dignity of the person.

What conclusions can be drawn from the first part of this study? First, today mainline Protestant and Roman Catholic teaching and theology support both religious liberty and human rights. Such support should help the practical struggle for human rights in our world and the effort to prevent religious intolerance from taking away human rights.

Second, historically religious liberty explicitly came to the fore of consciousness without great support from the Western Christian churches or theology. Institutional self-interest played an important role in the acceptance of religious liberty by the Christian churches. However, in time the Christian churches found resources in their own traditions to accept religious freedom and tolerance. If history is any lesson for the present, there is bad news here. One cannot expect churches themselves on the basis of their own teaching to be in the forefront of defending religious freedom and tolerance. Some religious bodies will probably continue to violate human rights in the name of religious truth. Other factors including the secularization of the state and plurality of religions will be much more important in bringing about the acceptance of religous freedom and tolerance in our world. One can, however, hope that the lessons of history will not repeat themselves.

II. Freedom and Human Rights within the Church

The subject of this second section on freedom and human rights within the Christian Church must be reduced dramatically. The first limit will be to focus only on the Roman Catholic Church. This choice and limitation are not merely arbitrary. From the practical viewpoint it would be impossible to consider all the different Protestant traditions and denominations. The Roman Catholic Church is clearly the largest single church. From a theoretical perspective Roman Catholicism has had much more difficulty dealing with the reality of freedom in general and with freedom in the church than mainline Protestant churches.[25] In addition, Roman Catholic ecclesiology by its very nature has more tensions in dealing with freedom because of its insistence on the chruch as a visible society with God-given authority and structure.

Also necessary is the recognition of the complexity involved in concepts such as freedom and human rights. Volumes have been written and even libraries filled on these subjects. Freedom, especially in the sense of freedom from, can never be an absolute in any society or community. By its very nature any society — political, cultural, or social — requires the members to work together for the good of the society. Human society in general and the state or political society in particular certainly cannot absolutize freedom to the exclusion of all other moral concerns and values. This is especially true of the social aspects of freedom that are bound to tread on the freedom of others. Libertarians do tend to absolutize the reality of freedom, but they recognize that limitations on individual freedom are necessary precisely because of the freedom of others. The United States has traditionally taken great pride in its support of human freedoms, but even religious freedom in the United States is limited. The United States does not allow Mormons to practice their belief in polygamy. The children of Jehovah's Witnesses who need blood transfusions are legally taken away from their parents who oppose such transfusions so they can obtain blood. Recently the Supreme Court declared that one had no absolute right to be free from work on one's religious days of observance. If freedom and even religious freedom are limited in secular society, freedom and religious freedom will be more limited in religious societies or more specifically in Christian churches. Here also "limits" are placed on the content of belief. The Christian Church is the community of disciples of Jesus who believe in the gospel message. Certain limits are involved in what it means to belong to the Christian Church. One is not free to deny certain beliefs and be Christian. At the same time, however, Christians as members of churches have many freedoms that should be protected. The Christian tradition itself has frequently appealed to the important Pauline notion of Christian freedom, but again no one holds that Christian freedom can be a justification to believe or to do whatever one might want.

The concept of basic human rights is likewise complex and has received great attention in recent years. Human rights is not a univocal term. Mention has already been made of the different understandings of human rights in liberal, socialist, and Third World countries. David Hollenbach distinguishes three different aspects of rights—personal, social, and instrumental—which would apply to all the different content matter of rights—religious, economic, political, and so on.[26] Again I do not think, especially in the area of social rights in practice, that one can speak of absolute or exceptionless rights. Here too in the social area my rights might conflict with the rights of others.[27] Thus in any discussion of freedom and human rights we need to underline the complexity of the concepts involved and to recognize that one can neither absolutize freedom nor absolutize rights in the social area.

Freedom and Human Rights in Roman Catholicism

In a true sense one can use the categories of freedom and human rights as tools to deal with very many of the tensions being experienced in the Roman Catholic Church today. Most of the internal problems experienced in the church stem from the tension between authority and freedom. What is the proper use of authority and what are proper roles of freedom? Some tension will always exist between authority, understood in the sense of a God-given authority entrusted to the church and in a specific way to certain officeholders in the church, and the freedom of the believers. However, a reduction of these tensions is possible.

From a theoretical viewpoint many contemporary Catholic theologians have attempted to rethink authority in the church in order to avoid the dangers of an overauthoritarianism which characterized pre-Vatican II Catholicism. The Constitution on Divine Revelation of the Second Vatican Council (par. 10) recognizes that teaching authority in the church serves the word of God and is governed by it. "This teaching office is not above the word of God but serves it, teaching only what has been handed on. . . ." Often in the past the question of authoritative church teaching was understood in two terms — authoritative church teaching and the conscience of the individual. Now the proper understanding requires three terms — the word of God, which both the authoritative church teaching office and the conscience of the believer, in different ways, try to discern.

A traditional Thomistic notion of authority also supports the above understanding. The Thomistic tradition has maintained an intrinsic and realistic approach which proposes that something is commanded because it is good. An extrinsic approach is voluntaristic and maintains something is good because it is commanded. For Aquinas, to command is to move another through intellect and will. Blind obedience has no place in a Thomistic understanding. Authority must conform itself to truth and not the other way around.[28]

A renewed ecclesiology shows the church is primarily the community of believers. All the baptized share in the threefold office of Jesus as priest, teacher, and sovereign. In addition to the role of all believers there is also the hierarchical role and function in the service of the community. Thus, the hierarchical teaching office is not totally identical with the whole teaching function in the church. The older distinction between the *Ecclesia docens* and the *Ecclesia discens* cannot be maintained today. The relationship of the hierarchical teaching office to the total church is much more complex than it was often thought to be in the past.

Contemporary Catholic eschatology stresses the imperfection of all existing reality in the light of the fullness of the reign of God. These eschatological considerations have affected the understanding of the church itself. The church is not the reign or kingdom of God as was taught in Catholic theology before Vatican II. The reign of God is much broader than the church, and the church always stands in judgment under the fullness of the reign of God. Future eschatological fullness reminds those existing in the present of the imperfection of all reality including the church. The church is no longer thought of as a perfect society but as a pilgrim community.

Epistemological considerations indicate that the search for truth is much more complicated and arduous than was assumed to be the case in the past. Historical consciousness, with its emphasis on the particular, the individual, and the contingent, has replaced an older classicism which stressed the eternal, the immutable, and the unchanging. Historical consciousness, properly understood, charts a middle course between classicism and sheer existentialism. Historical consciousness involves a more tentative epistemology and recognizes the role and importance of more inductive methodologies. One of the most startling statements accepting historical consciousness is found in *Octogesima adveniens*, the letter of Paul VI issued in 1971 on the eightieth anniversary of Leo XIII's groundbreaking encyclical *Rerum novarum*. "In the face of such widely varying situations it is difficult for us to utter a unified message and to put forward a solution which has universal validity. Such is not our ambition, nor is it our mission. It is up to the Christian communities to analyze with objectivity the situation which is proper to their own country, to shed on it the light of the gospel's unalterable words and to draw principles of reflection, norms of judgment and directions for action from the social teaching of the church."[29]

Historical consciousness recognizes the existence of and need for theological pluralism. No longer can the perennial theology and philosophy serve as the only way of trying to understand God's saving truth. Naturally pluralism has its limits, but the need to recognize and even promote theological pluralism in the church also is present.

All of these factors have influenced the theoretical understanding of authority in the Catholic Church and of teaching authority in particular. The concept of infallibility has been challenged by a few and reinterpreted by many, but infallibility as such does not have much practical significance in the daily life of the members of the church. In the more practically significant area of authoritative or authentic, noninfallible teaching, the possibility of dissent within the church exists. Many people in reality are acting on the basis of such dissent, so that it is having a practical effect on the life of the church. However, at the present time the hierarchical officeholders in the church have been very reluctant in any way to accept and countenance the reality of dissent.

In accord with Catholic ecclesiology two levels to every question concerning the church are present — the theoretical understanding and the institutional and practical structures corresponding to the theoretical understanding. Official church teaching itself and contemporary theologians have proposed many newer understandings of the role of the church and of church authority, but little or no change in actual ecclesial structures correspond with this newer theoretical outlook.

Catholic social teaching in its attempt to favor both personalism and communitarianism, while avoiding the dangers of individualism and collectivism, has insisted on the importance of the principle of subsidiarity. According to this principle, as explained in greater detail in the preceding chapter, the higher and more centralized structures are a *subsidium*, or help, to do those things that cannot be done adequately on lower and less centralized bureaucratic levels.[30] The theoretical understanding of the church as the people of God involving a community of equals in the discipleship of Jesus with special teaching, ruling, and sanctifying offices existing on local, regional, national, and worldwide levels provides the basis for the application of the principle of subsidiarity throughout the life of the church. Unfortunately few structural modifications involving the principle of subsidiarity are evident even in the new Code of Canon Law that has just been promulgated for the Latin church. Authority remains highly centralized and without mechanisms geared to institutionalize the newer theological understandings.[31]

One important theoretical aspect of subsidiarity as applied to the church is the principle of collegiality involving the college of bishops functioning together. National and regional conferences of bishops are one institutional illustration of collegiality, but they have been very limited in what they can do. The Synod of Bishops is another instrumentality created after Vatican II, but the synods that have taken place have been heavily controlled by Rome and have not really been a free exercise of collegial participation by the college of bishops throughout the world. Collegiality is badly in need of structures that can make it a reality. It is probably safe to say that true collegiality will not exist until a group of bishops can publicly express their differences with the bishop of Rome, who holds the Petrine office in the church. The gross inadequacies of the structures set up to mirror subsidiarity and collegiality well illustrate the fact that church structures are badly needed to carry out the theoretical understandings agreed upon at Vatican II, to say nothing of further theological developments. In this connection we must recall that structures will never totally solve such tensions, for tensions will always be present between saving truth and freedom, between church community and individual liberty. In addition, perfect structures can never exist. However, at the present time all must acknowledge that the existing structures are woefully inadequate in mediating even the theological understandings already recognized in official Catholic teaching.

Just as freedom in the church can be a way of dealing with most of the major problems facing the internal life of the church today, so the language of rights can be used as an instrument to deal with the major tensions facing the contemporary church. Rights language is the strongest ethical language that exists precisely because it makes a claim on other people to do something. Value language, for example, is not nearly as strong. It is not surprising that in the contemporary church people are using the language of rights to make their claims. Thus, for example, The Charter of the Rights of Catholics in the Church speaks about the right to dissent, the right for all to embrace marriage or celibacy, the right to decide in conscience the size of families and the appropriate method of family planning, the rights of the divorced and remarried to the sacraments, the right of Catholic women to the exercise of all the powers of the church, and so on. Basically this document uses the format of the charter of rights to propose a blueprint for how the church should be renewed.[32] We could not possibly deal adequately with such a charter in one scholarly article, for one would have to examine individually each of the rights proposed. Yet we can see how some have used the concepts of freedom and of human rights to deal with most of the internal questions facing the church today. This study can only point out a few of the theological changes that have occurred and the lack of existing structures to mediate these newer understandings. Naturally a difference of opinion exists on how much should be done, but I have just made the minimum point that even the officially accepted changes in theological understanding have not been fleshed out in appropriate institutional structures.

Fundamental Rights of Roman Catholics

The remainder of this study will concentrate on the question of the fundamental rights of members of the Catholic Church.[33] The new Code of Canon Law has a section on the fundamental rights and obligations of Catholics.[34] By its definition a list of fundamental rights or a bill of rights does not intend to be a detailed spelling out of all rights or a blueprint for governing the entire society. The first part of this study has mentioned the Universal Declaration of Human Rights of The United Nations which contains only thirty articles. Many countries have adopted similar rights in their own constitutions.

As pointed out in the first part, Roman Catholicism has become a staunch supporter of human dignity, human freedom, and fundamental human rights in the political and social orders. Justice in the World, the document of the 1971 Synod of Bishops, stressed the mission of the church in defending and promoting the dignity, freedom, and the fundamental rights of human beings. Yet the church itself must first strive to be just in its own community if it is to speak about justice to others. This document then examines the modes of acting and lifestyle of the church and proposes what could be called a bill of rights for members of the church. Within the church rights must be preserved — the right to a decent wage, rights of women to a share of responsibility and participation, right to suitable freedom of expression, rights of the accused, right to some share in determining and deciding what is done.[35]

The 1974 Synod of Bishops reiterated the same basic message. The church recognizes that its mission on behalf of promoting human rights in the world obliges it to a constant examination and an increasing purification of its own life, legislation, structures, and plan of action. Within the church itself violations of human rights must be denounced.[36] Other official church documents make the same basic point.[37]

In the light of this background one can only be astounded at what is found under the rubric "The Obligations and Rights of All Christian Faithful" embracing canons 208-223 in Book II of the new Code of Canon Law. The fundamental rights presented there are totally inadequate. The rights and obligations are mixed together in the space of sixteen canons. Eighteen different rights are mentioned in this section, but the inadequacies of the section on rights are glaring and manifold.

First of all the tendency is to avoid as much as possible any mention of freedom. The first canon (208) asserts an equality with regard to dignity and action in the church, but no mention is made of the freedom of the Christian. Freedom appears only twice in those canons (215 and 278) dealing with freely founding associations and the freedom of inquiry for scholars.

Freedom must play a much more central role in the theoretical understanding of the rights of Christians, to say nothing about the practical implementation of these rights. From a uniquely Christian perspective Christian freedom is an important part of the faith tradition. Granted, as has been frequently stressed in these pages, freedom cannot be absolutized and can surely be abused; but it cannot be forgotten or left out. One of the primary functions of the church and its laws is to protect, defend, empower, and encourage true Christian freedom.

Recent Catholic social teaching has emphasized basic human rights, grounding them in the dignity of the human person and stressing the fundamental importance of the freedom of the human person. But in the section on fundamental rights in the Code of Canon Law the freedom of the believer in the church is hardly mentioned. A great fear of even using the word freedom seems present. Compare the approach to freedom found in the fundamental rights of Christians in the new code with the role of freedom in a report on due process received by the American bishops in 1969 from a committee of the Canon Law Society of America. The bishops' conference recommended that the procedures found in this document be used by individual bishops in their diocese. In their resolution the bishops maintained, "The promotion of adequate protection of human rights and freedoms within the church is central to the bishops' role of service to the people of God."[38] This report begins with a preamble proposing the "conviction that all persons in the church are fundamentally equal in regard to their common rights and freedoms" and then spells out what could be called a bill of rights specifically indicating the fundamental rights and freedoms of people in the church.[39]

Second, the enunciation of the fundamental rights in this section of the new code is severely weakened by mixing together rights and duties and by qualifying the rights to such an extent that they fail to serve their real purpose. For example, the first canon (208) speaks about the genuine equality of all in the church but quickly adds a reference to inequality based on condition and office in the church. The second canon in the series (209) states the obligation to preserve communion with the church at all times. The fifth canon (212) calls for obedience to the sacred pastors.

Compare this approach with the enumeration of the rights of the members of the church given by the 1971 Synod of Bishops and with the enumeration of human rights in general given by Pope John XXIII in *Pacem in terris*. In both cases the rights are not mixed together with obligations, and the rights are not qualified and limited. Unfortunately the framers of the new code are out of tune with other church documents. In addition the framers of the new code did not take to heart the criticism made by a committee of the Canon Law Society of America concerning the first draft of rights proposed for a fundamental law of the church in 1969. This committee pointed out the excessive limitations and qualifications of the rights proposed in the original schema.[40]

Third, this section of the code basically relies upon a pre-Vatican II ecclesiology that sees the church primarily as a hierarchical structure and not as the people of God. The basic dignity, freedom, equality, and participative rights of all must first be stressed. The code contains later sections on laity, clerics, bishops, religious, and so on. These distinctions should not be brought into an explanation of what is common to all in the church. It is more than ironic that the very last canon in the section (223) maintains that ecclesiastical authority is entitled to regulate, in view of the common good, the exercise of rights that are proper to Christ's faithful. The ecclesiology at work in this section prevents it from being a declaration of the fundamental rights and freedoms of all believers in the church. By bringing into this section the hierarchical differences within the church the framers have also logically called for many limitations on the rights mentioned.

Fourth, the final version of fundamental rights proclaimed in the new code is even more disappointing because it is actually a regression from what was found in the schema proposed in 1977.[41] For example, canon 17 in the proposed schema ruled out discrimination on the basis of descent, nationality, social condition, or sex; but there is no explicit mention of this in the new Code. Canon 34 in the 1977 schema recognized the possible abuse of authority and power in the church and assured the faithful a proper redress. No mention of the abuse of authority is made in this section of the new code. Also the earlier schema for canon 36 spelled out some of the due process procedures that should be found in the church — the right to know the names of one's accuser, the right to hear the reasons for judgments given. These are not mentioned in the section of the new code. It should be noted that even the 1977 schema does not mention the right not to incriminate oneself. Note too that the 1977 schema does not contain a final canon affirming that ecclesiastical authority may regulate the exercise of all these rights.

Fifth, from a practical viewpoint the most serious flaw in this section on rights is the failure to mention enlarged possibilities of administrative courts in the case of the violation of rights. The reason for such a lack in this section is the fact that the section on processes in the seventh book of the new code makes no mention of the existence of administrative tribunals. All the preliminary schemata had provided for the possibility of such administrative tribunals on the diocesan, regional, and national levels, but the new code left them out.[42]

The administrative tribunals were originally proposed as an easily available remedy for the violation of rights by administrative action. The 1969 report of a committee of the Canon Law Society of America dealing with due process pointed out that the administrative area of church governance has lately experienced the greatest growth. Think for example of the creation of many new governing boards, departments, and agencies to supplement the bishop's personal administrative activities. Examples of these recent developments include personnel boards, liturgical commissions, parish councils, and so on. Here the rights of many people need to be protected. In the old code the only recourse against administrative decisions of bishops is to the sacred congregations in Rome, but such a process rendered such recourse practically unavailable to most people. To protect the rights of the faithful the American bishops on the suggestion of the committee of the Canon Law Society recommended that individual bishops adopt the procedures proposed for conciliation (mediated dialogue), arbitration (voluntary referral to an impartial referee), and for better ways of structuring administrative decisions in order to avoid unjust actions before they occur. The report also looked forward to the coming into existence of administrative tribunals in the forthcoming Code of Canon Law.[43]

The American canonists at that time and canonists in general until the final appearance of the new code had every reason to believe that such administrative tribunals would be sanctioned by the new code. The commission for the revision of the code and the Synod of Bishops in 1967 called for the new code to set up a series of administrative tribunals in the church and to evolve proper canonical procedures at each level for the protection of rights.[44] Pope Paul VI mentioned in 1977 that the new code would have administrative tribunals.[45] All the proposed schemata before the final version of the code included provisions for administrative tribunals. Their absence in the final document greatly weakens the practical defense of rights in the church.

One of the advantages of administrative tribunals would be to recognize in practice the existence of the separation of powers, so that an independent judiciary would function. The separation of powers has been looked upon as essential to real due process. Too often in the past on the local level the bishop has been both legislator or administrator and judge. Due process requires that the authority in question be subject to independent judicial review. One of the many criticisms of the present inadequate procedures of the Congregation for the Doctrine of the Faith in dealing with theologians whose writings are suspect is that the congregation is both the accuser and the judge.[46]

This analysis shows the very inadequate nature of the fundamental rights of members of the church found in the new Code of Canon Law. Our analysis also bears out the suspicion raised in the first part of the study about the hesitancy to recognize freedom and its protection as an important value in the church. Recall that in the discussion on religious liberty a tendency on the part of some was to base the argument for the existence of religious liberty on the nature of civil constitutional government and not on theological and ethical values of freedom as such. Such an approach in itself can imply, and can be used by others to maintain, that such freedoms and rights should not be found in the church. In the light of this reluctance it is necessary to indicate why freedom and basic human rights must be found in the church too.

The argument is heard that the church is a different type of society from the state. Freedom and fundamental rights exist in the state to protect the individual from the power of the state, but the church is a community which cannot be adversarial to the good of the individual members. Others maintain that the church by its very nature is an authoritative society understood as the authority of God shared by human beings. Such an understanding of the church is incompatible with the recognition of the freedoms of its members. However, these reasons in my judgment do not deny the need for legitimate freedom and its protection in the church.

Freedom is not just a secular value but is a truly Christian and human value. The freedom of the Christian is a very important Christian concept developed especially by St. Paul. Freedom and liberation are important Christian realities which should have ramifications in all areas of the Christian's existence. The concept of freedom in civil societies is not based primarily on the nature of the state but rather on the dignity of the human person. Baptism and membership in the church do not take away one's basic human dignity and all that flows from it. The Catholic theological tradition has rightly given great importance to the human and in fact sees the Christian not as destroying the human but rather as the fulfillment of the human. Whatever is rooted in the dignity of the human person must be respected in the church.

It is true that civil political society and the church are not exactly the same. What is true and proper for the state will not necessarily be true and proper for the church. However, an analogy exists between the two and not total opposition. Since freedom and fundamental rights are based on human dignity, they must be found in both the church and the state but in somewhat different ways. A contemporary Catholic ecclesiology no longer sees the church primarily as a hierarchical pyramid but as the people of God. The hierarchical office is at the service of the community of equal disciples. Within the church abuses of power can readily be present, and the members of the church need to be protected against such possible abuses. As discussed above, freedom is never an absolute, but the church must acknowledge and protect the freedom and the fundamental human rights that flow from the dignity of the human person. Official church statements in the area of social justice have recognized the need for freedom and basic human rights in the church, but for some reason these realities are not present in the new Code of Canon Law to the extent that they should be.

In conclusion, four basic steps are necessary to insure that the church and its law recognize and protect fundamental human rights and freedom in the church. More work needs to be done on all these levels, but this study has tried to make some contribution to this ongoing task.

The first step is to insist on the need for and importance of such freedom and rights in the church. The second step is to elucidate the proper grounding and basis for ecclesial rights. In my judgment such rights should be based on the dignity of the human person as known through reason, experience, and revelation and on the fact of baptism.[47] The third step is to develop a theoretical model of what the fundamental rights of church members should be. Since other authors and groups have proposed such models, the present study did not go into this important task. Fourth, practical procedures must be put in place to institutionalize and protect these fundamental ecclesial rights.

In summary this study has addressed the problem of religious freedom and human rights from some Christian perspectives. The first part indicated how the mainline Protestant and Catholic traditions gradually came to accept religious liberty but only after the concept came to the fore through other agencies. This historical analysis might indicate some ways in which the struggles for religious freedom in our contemporary world can be helped. The second part moved from the area of the world to the area of the church and concentrated on how the Roman Catholic Church in its internal life tries to deal with the freedom and basic human rights of its members. Contemporary Roman Catholicism needs to adopt structures and institutions which better protect the freedom and human rights of the believers.

NOTES

1. *Human Rights: A Compilation of International Instruments* (United Nations Publications, 1983, Sales No. E. 83 XIV. 1).

2. In the best sense of the term tolerance seems to refer primarily to the moral sphere, whereas religious liberty refers rather to the social and juridical areas. In addition tolerance has been used in the Roman Catholic tradition as something much less than religious liberty. While recognizing these significant differences, it is not impossible for practical purposes to use the words interchangeably.

3. For the documentation from the early meetings of the World Council of Churches beginning in Amsterdam in 1948 and for a discussion of religious liberty in the light of World Council of Churches' deliberations, see A. F. Carrillo de Albornoz, *The Basis of Religious Liberty* (New York: Association Press, 1963). Declaration on Religious Freedom in Walter Abbott, ed., *The Documents of Vatican II* (New York: Guild Press, 1966), pp. 675-700.

4. A. F. Carrillo de Albornoz, *Religious Liberty* (New York: Sheed and Ward, 1967), pp. 3-24. Carrillo, who was head of the World Council of Churches' Secretariate on Religious Liberty, wrote this volume as a commentary and analysis of the Declaration on Religious Freedom of the Second Vatican Council.

5. For these statements and commentaries on them consult the following works: Pontifical Commission, *Justitia et Pax, The Church and Human Rights* (Vatican City: Vatican Polyglot Press, 1975); Allen O. Miller, ed., *A Christian Delcaration on Human Rights* (Grand Rapids, MI: Eerdmans, 1977); Jørgen Lissner and Arne Sovik, eds., *A Lutheran Reader on Human Rights* (Geneva: Lutheran World Federation, 1977); Alan D. Falconer, ed., *Understanding Human Rights: An*

nterdisciplinary and Interfaith Study (Dublin: Irish School of Ecumenics, 1980); Arlene Swidler, ed., *Human Rights in Religious Traditions* (New York: Pilgrim, 1982); this symposium originally appeared in *Journal of Ecumenical Studies* 19 (Summer 1982): pp. 1-113, special pagination. For a small pamphlet containing the significant bibliography see Alan Falconer, *What to Read on Human Rights* (London: British Council of Churches, 1980).

6. Thomas G. Sanders, *Protestant Concepts of Church and State* (Garden City, NY: Doubleday Anchor Books, 1965), p. 15.

7. Ibid., pp. 330ff; Philip Wogaman, *Protestant Faith and Religious Liberty* (Nashville: Abingdon Press, 1967), pp. 42, 43.

8. Paul Tillich, *The Protestant Era* (Chicago: University of Chicago Press, 1948), especially pp. xii-xxix.

9. Wogaman, *Protestant Faith and Religious Liberty*, pp. 109-115.

10. For a contemporary, systematic Protestant approach to freedom see Peter C. Hodgson, *New Birth of Freedom: A Theology of Bondage and Liberation* (Philadelphia: Fortress, 1976).

11. James M. Gustafson, *Protestant and Roman Catholic Ethics: Prospects for Rapprochement* (Chicago: University of Chicago Press, 1978), pp. 30-94.

12. John F. Cronin, *Social Principles and Economic Life*, rev. ed. (Milwaukee: Bruce, 1965), pp. 218ff.

13. Sanders, *Protestant Concepts*, pp. 262-274.

14. Reinhold Niebuhr, *The Children of Light and the Children of Darkness* (New York: Scribners, 1944), p. xi.

15. Helpful studies of this historical development include the following: Roger Aubert, "Liberalism and the Church in the Nineteenth Century," in Joseph Masson et al., *Tolerance and the Catholic* (New York: Sheed and Ward, 1955), pp. 47-76; Fr. Refoulé, "L'Église et les libertés de Léon XIII à Jean XXIII," *Le Supplément* 125 (mai 1978): 243-259; Bernard Plongeron, "L'Église et les Declarations des droits de l'homme au XVIIIe siècle," *Nouvelle Revue Théologique* 101 (1979): 358-377; Jean-Marie Aubert, "Les droits de l'homme interpellent les églises," *Le Supplément* 141 (mai 1982): 149-179; Ch. Wachenheim, "Comprendre l'attitude de l'Église," *Le Supplément* 141 (mai 1982): 237-248.

16. Aubert, "Les droits de l'homme," p. 59.

17. Pope John XXIII, *Mater et magistra*, par. 212, in *Renewing the Earth: Catholic Documents on Peace, Justice, and Liberation*, ed. David J. O'Brien and Thomas A. Shannon (Garden City, NY: Doubleday Image Books, 1977), p. 102.

18. Pope John XXIII, *Pacem in terris*, par. 35, in O'Brien and Shannon, *Renewing the Earth*, p. 132.

19. For Murray's discussion of this issue see John Courtney Murray, *The Problem of Religious Freedom* (Westminster, MD: Newman Press, 1965), especially pp. 19-22.

20. Murray himself even in 1966 strongly urged a greater freedom in the church. John Courtney Murray, "Freedom, Authority, Community," *America* 115 (December 3, 1966): 734-741.

21. See, for example, Sixth Assembly WCC at Vancouver, "Statement on Human Rights," *Ecumenical Review* 36 (1984): 87-91; Otfried Höffe, et al., *Jean Paul II et les droits de l'homme* (Fribourg: Editions Universitaires, 1980).

22. In addition to the bibliography mentioned, the following articles are helpful in describing the approach to human rights in Protestantism: Roger Mehl, "La tradition protestante et les droits de l'homme," *Revue d'histoire et de philosophie réligieuses* 58 (1978): 367-377; Th. Tschuy, "Le protestantisme et les problèmes théologiques de droits de l'homme," *Le Supplément* 141 (mai 1982): 221-237.

23. Jürgen Moltmann, *On Human Dignity: Political Theology and Ethics* (Philadelphia: Fortress Press, 1984), especially pp. 3-58; Max L. Stackhouse, "A Protestant Perspective on the Woodstock Human Rights Project," in *Human Rights in the Americas: The Struggle for Consensus*, ed. Alfred Hennelly and John Langan (Washington, DC, Georgetown University Press, 1982), pp. 142-158.

24. Pope Paul VI, *Octogesima adveniens*, par. 22; O'Brien and Shannon, *Renewing the Earth*, p. 364.

25. For some discussion of the question of rights within Protestant churches see U. Scheuner, "Les droits de l'homme à l'interieur des Églises protestantes," *Revue d'histoire et de philosophie religieuses* 58 (1978): 379-397; Norbert Greinacher, "For Freedom Christ Has Set Us Free," *Cross Currents* 31 (1982): 185-193; Patrick J. Colgan, "The Protection of Ecclesial Rights in Other Churches: An Ecumenical Survey," forthcoming in *The Jurist*.

26. David Hollenbach, *Claims in Conflict: Retrieving and Renewing the Catholic Human Rights Tradition* (New York: Paulist, 1979), pp. 95-100.

27. John Langan, "Defining Human Rights: A Revision of the Liberal Tradition," in *Human Rights in the Americas: The Struggle for Consensus*, ed. Alfred Hennelly and John Langan (Washington, DC: Georgetown University Press, 1982), pp. 69-101.

28. Jean-Marie Aubert, *Loi de Dieu, lois des hommes* (Tournai, Belgium: Desclée, 1964).

29. Pope Paul VI, *Octogesima adveniens*, par. 4; O'Brien and Shannon, *Renewing the Earth*, pp. 353, 354.

30. For a contemporary understanding and use of this princi-

ple see U.S. bishops' pastoral (First Draft), "Catholic Social Teaching and the U.S. Economy," *Origins* 14 (November 15, 1984): 355.

31. Before the publication of the new Code of Canon Law severe criticisms were made of the proposed *Lex Fundamentalis* which was never promulgated as such. However, many of those criticisms are still applicable to the new code itself. See Canon Law Society of America Task Force Subcommittee on the *Lex Fundamentalis*, "A General Analysis of the Proposed Schema on the *Lex Fundamentalis*," *Canon Law Society of America Proceedings* 32 (1970): 29-46; "A Critique of the Revised Schema of the *Lex Fundamentalis*," *Canon Law Society of America Proceedings* 33 (1971): 65-77; Giuseppe Alberigo et al., *Legge e Vangelo: Discussione su una Legge fondamentale per la Chiesa* (Brescia: Paideia, 1972).

32. Association for the Rights of Catholics in the Church, *Charter of the Rights of Catholics in the Church*. This pamphlet is available from the association at P.O. Box 3932, Philadelphia, PA 19146. For some similar statements see Greinacher, *Cross Currents* 31 (1932): 185-193; Greinacher and Jens, *Freiheitsrechte für Christen?*, pp. 39-79.

33. There is also a large bibliography dealing with this subject including the following: James A. Coriden, ed., *We, The People of God . . . A Study of Constitutional Government for the Church*, (Huntington, IN: Our Sunday Visitor, 1968); James A. Coriden, ed., *The Case for Freedom: Human Rights in the Church* (Washington, DC: Corpus, 1969); Johannes Neumann, *Menschenrechte—Auch in der Kirche?* (Zürich: Benziger, 1976); Norbert Greinacher and Inge Jens, eds., *Freiheitsrechte für Christen? Warum die Kirche ein Grundgesetz braucht* (München: R. Piper, 1980); Eugenio Corecco et al., eds., *Les Droits Fondamentaux du Chrétien dans l'Église et dans la société* (Fribourg: Editions Universitaires, 1981). This 1,328-page volume is the proceedings of the Fourth International Congress of Canon Law held in Fribourg in 1980. Helpful articles include the following: James A. Coriden, "Human Rights in the Church: A Matter of Credibility and Authenticity," in *The Church and the Rights of Man* (Concilium 124), ed. Alois Müller and Norbert Greinacher (New York: Seabury Press, 1979); Frederick R. McManus, "Human Rights in the Church," in Falconer, *Understanding Human Rights*, pp. 114-132; James H. Provost, "Ecclesial Rights," *Canon Law Society of America Proceedings* 44 (1982): 41-62.

34. *Codex Iuris Canonici* (Vatican City: Editrice Vaticana, 1983), *The Code of Canon Law: In English Translation* (Grand Rapids: Eerdmans, 1983), canons 208-223.

35. O'Brien and Shannon, *Renewing the Earth*, p. 400.

36. 1974 Synod of Bishops, "Statement on Human Rights and Reconciliation," *Origins* 4 (November 7, 1974): 318, 319.

37. Jean Bernhard, "Les droits fondamentaux dans la perspective de la *Lex fundamentalis* et de la revision du Code de Droit Canonique," in Corecco, *Les Droits Fondamentaux*, pp. 374-376.

38. *On Due Process* (Washington: National Conference of Catholic Bishops, 1969), p. 2.

39. *On Due Process*, pp. 4, 5.

40. *Canon Law Society of America Proceedings* 32 (1970): 39.

41. *Schema Canonum Libri II: De Populo Dei* (Vatican City: Vatican Polyglot Press, 1977). A translation was made in English and widely circulated by the National Conference of Catholic Bishops.

42. For a complete discussion of administrative tribunals see Kevin Matthews, *The Development and Future of the Administrative Tribunal*, which is published in its entirety in *Studia Canonica* 18 (1984): 1-233. Also see Thomas E. Molloy, "Administrative Recourse in the Proposed Code of Canon Law," *Canon Law Society of America Proceedings* 44 (1982): 263-273.

43. *On Due Process*, pp. 11-15.

44. *Communicationes* 2 (1969): 82, 83.

45. Paulus VI, "Ad Praelatos Auditores et Officiales Tribunalis Sacrae Romanae Rotae," *Acta Apostolicae Sedis* 69 (1977): 152.

46. Neumann, *Menschenrecte*, pp. 126-153.

47. There has been much discussion about the grounding or basis of human rights for the Christian. For a summary and analysis of the literature in this area see Gustave Thils, *Droits de l'homme et perspectives chrétiennes* (Louvain-la-Neuve: F. Peeters, 1981), pp. 49-96.

8: An Analysis of the United States Bishops' Pastoral Letter on the Economy

This chapter will discuss the question of how the pastoral letter of the United States bishops relates religious ethical inquiry to economic policy. In other words, the study will deal principally with the moral-theological methodology employed in the letter. A proper evaluation must consider the methodology in this letter in the light of recent developments in Catholic moral theology and social ethics. This discussion will examine the question of theological ethical methodology from four perspectives — presuppositions, theological contexts, the different levels of ethical discourse, and an unresolved tension.

I. Presuppositions

The first presupposition concerns the justification of the church's involvement in the discussion of the economy. Many object that the church and theology should not be involved in economic matters. The church has no competency in this area and therefore should stay out of it.

Throughout its history the Catholic Church in one way or another has addressed the problems involved in life in this world, including the economic aspects of human existence. Beginning with the encyclical *Rerum novarum* of Leo XIII in 1891, a body of official Catholic Church teachings with regard to social and economic questions has come into existence. The economic situation of the late nineteenth century with the spread of laissez-faire capitalism and the response of Marx-

ism called for a response from the churches. Within Protestantism the social gospel movement came into existence at
this time. Official Catholic social teaching has continued to
be developed and proposed by subsequent popes, the Second
Vatican Council, and the Synod of Bishops. Yet the reason
for such church involvement in social and economic issues,
has recently undergone a significant shift in the Roman Catholic perspective. Before the Second Vatican Council (1965)
two reasons were usually proposed to justify the church's involvement. The church was interested in the material world
because a sufficiency of the goods of this world was necessary
in order for people to live a spiritual life. In addition, the
church has the mission to teach her members to live properly
in this world and to obey God's law in order to obtain their
eternal salvation.[1]

Before Vatican II Catholic theology generally accepted the
basic goodness and importance of the natural realm of life
in this world but saw this as the bottom floor of a two-story
universe, with the supernatural order on top. A duality or
even dichotomy existed between the supernatural, where grace
and the gospel primarily operated, and the natural, where
reason and natural law pointed out how human beings should
live in this world. In this understanding the church itself had
a twofold mission — divinization in the supernatural order and
humanization in the natural order.

At Vatican II and since a studied attempt grew to overcome this duality and to relate the gospel, faith, and grace
directly to life in this world and the so-called natural order.
"This split between the faith which many profess and their
daily lives deserves to be counted among the more serious errors of our age."[2] The Pastoral Constitution on the Church
in the Modern World also employed a methodology which
tried to relate the gospel and faith more directly to the problems of life in the modern world. The earlier papal social encyclicals (even Pope John XXIII's *Pacem in terris* in 1963)
employed a natural law methodology which discussed how
Christians are to act in this world on the basis of the laws
governing human relationships which God the creator has
written into human nature. The earlier approach saw all of

social, political, and economic life in this world in the light
of the natural law and did not appeal directly and explicitly
to the gospel, redemption, grace, or Jesus Christ.[3]

Since Vatican II official Catholic social teaching has continued and extended the effort to relate the gospel and faith
directly to the daily life of Christians in this world. The gospel
must penetrate and affect every aspect of human existence.
The 1971 Synod of Bishops succinctly summarized the new
approach: "Action on behalf of justice and participation in
the transformation of the world fully appear to us as a constitutive dimension of the preaching of the gospel, or, in other
words, of the church's mission for the redemption of the human
race and its liberation from every oppressive situation."[4] In
the light of this understanding only one mission of the church
is now present — the mission of evangelization that includes
as a constitutive dimension action on behalf of justice and the
transformation of the world. Attempts have been made to back
down from this statement, but no sentence from a recent
church document has been quoted more frequently than this
passage. One can have magnificent liturgy, great preaching,
and a marvelous internal community life, but without a social
mission one does not have church or the gospel. This changed
understanding explains the strong commitment of the contemporary Catholic Church in general, and for our purposes
the United States Catholic Church in particular, to the work
of social justice. If the church does not become involved in
social transformation, it has betrayed the gospel and its own
redemptive mission.

A further question, then, immediately arises: How do the
gospel, faith, and grace relate to the complex social and economic realities of the modern world? In my judgment the most
characteristic aspect of Catholic theology in general and moral
theology in particular is the acceptance of mediation. Revelation is mediated through scripture and tradition. The mystery
of God is mediated through Jesus, the visible institution of
the church, and the human realities of the sacramental liturgical system. Even the older Catholic approach to morality
did not appeal directly to God, because God's plan was mediated in and through the natural law undersood as human rea-

son directing human beings to their end in accord with their nature.

In the present context mediation means that the gospel, faith, and grace cannot deny or go around the human but are mediated in and through the human. The gospel does not provide a shortcut which avoids the human and supplies rather direct and easy answers to complex social problems. The gospel must be mediated in and through the human, human experience, and the human sciences. One cannot address these complex issues without knowledge of the social sciences, human experience, and all the other data involved in the situation itself. One cannot go directly from the gospel or from one scripture quotation to a specific ethical conclusion in a complex economic issue. Thus, for example, one cannot immediately conclude from the gospel imperative to come to the assistance of the poor that private ownership and capitalism are immoral.

The proper understanding of mediation avoids two opposite errors. On the one hand, some maintain that church teaching and theology have no competency in making judgments about economic issues. The Christian Church and Christian theology can only go so far as their uniquely Christian warrants will take them, which are often described as the principles expressing Christian love. Christian love, however, has no specific competency to solve complex economic issues. The opposite stance maintains that on the basis of the gospel and faith one can with ease and great certitude arrive at concrete solutions to complex ethical problems. Through some type of ethical or theological intuitionism the Christian can readily discern what is the will and the concrete act of God in these particular and specific circumstances.

Christian love and the gospel can and should become incarnate in the complex issues of economic structures and policies, but only in and through the human with all the limitations involved in the human as such. The gospel and faith should extend down to the specific and the concrete, but in so doing, the faith perspectives cannot claim to arrive at a certitude that is beyond the human possibilities. Faith and gospel values should affect specific decisions in the economic realm, but these decisions also depend heavily on the complex data and the scientific theories involved. Specifically Christian ideals and values must be brought to bear, but the final decision must mediate these aspects in and through all the relevant data and theories.

In this view the final specific judgment is truly a Christian, a human, and an ethical decision, but with heavy data from economics and the other sciences involved. However, it is not merely a technical economic decision. The Christian and human ethical decision must take into consideration all the other aspects that enter into a decision — the psychological, the sociological, the hygienic, the economic, the political, and so on — but the final decision is truly a Christian, human, and ethical decision and not merely a sociological or economic judgment.

Without explicitly adverting to the characteristic Catholic acceptance of mediation, the United States bishops' pastoral letter on the economy as well as the preceding one on peace illustrates this basic approach. They not only talk about the principles to govern social questions, but they descend to the level of particular and specific judgments. In making these judgments they have attempted to evaluate all the data involved, and they recognize that these judgments cannot claim a certitude that excludes the possibility of error. Other believing Christians in the church can arrive at different judgments and still belong to the same church. The church in fidelity to its own gospel vision must speak and work for justice in the economic realm, but on specific issues and policies a legitimate pluralism of approaches exists. The very justification of the church's involvement in such issues leads to the question of the methodology used by the church in addressing these issues.

A second presupposition of the pastoral letter which also has significant methodological ramifications concerns the audience to be addressed by the bishops. Here again the letter on the economy follows the approach of the earlier letter on peace. The bishops address two audiences. They seek to furnish guidance for members of their own church, and at the same time they want to add their voice to the public policy debate about the directions which the United States economy should take. The letter recognizes that in speaking to one's fellow believers appeals will be made to specifically Christian warrants, whereas often in addressing the public policy aspect the letter refrains from invoking specifically Christian warrants and appeals to common humanity, experience, and reason which are shared by all. The letter thus adopts the practical approach of addressing both audiences, but it leaves open the deeper and more theoretical question about the relationship between the Christian moral order and the human moral order. Are these two different moral orders, or is there just one moral order? The letter properly avoids dealing with the more theoretical question, but some short discussion of this important issue is called for here. The following paragraphs will summarize briefly what was developed in the third chapter.

In the older understanding prevalent before Vatican II the question as such never arose. In that perspective all of social life in the world was governed by a natural law that was the same for all human beings whether they were Christian or not. The question arose once great emphasis was put on the need for a distinctively Christian approach to social issues. What is the relationship between the distinctively Christian approach and the purely human approach? Perhaps the most adequate way to phrase the question for our present purposes is as follows: "Is there one social moral order for Christians and another for those who are not Christian?" My response to this question has been to affirm that there is only one social moral order that is the same for Christians and non-Christians. Such an answer is grounded in the fact that only one *de facto* historical order exists in which God wills to call all humankind to share in God's own love and life. The traditional Catholic understanding that grace brings the human to the fullness of human perfection supports this same conclusion.

The discussion began in this country with the question of the existence of a distinctively Christian ethic. Subsequent debate has, in my judgment, helped to clarify the real question — Is there a unique Christian moral order which differs from the human moral order existing for all others who are not

Christian? Many people, myself included, deny the existence of a unique Christian morality. Notice that the discussion is limited to the morality required of all Christians or of all humans as such and not to specific calls or vocations within a particular community. It is not necessary to go further into the discussion at the present time.[5]

The thesis that there is only one social moral order common to Christians and all others furnishes a strong theoretical basis for the fact that the pastoral letter can address two different audiences at the same time without involving itself in any inherent contradictions. The letter itself properly avoids the more theoretical issue and merely recognizes that it is speaking to two different audiences. Such a practice, however, is much more acceptable in light of the theory proposed above.

II. Theological Contexts

Two very important theological contexts are necessary to understand both the methodology and some of the conclusions of the pastoral letter on the economy — eschatology and ecclesiology. It might be only sheer coincidence, but the second drafts of the earlier pastoral on peace and of the later pastoral letter on the economy both gave more importance to eschatology than the first drafts.[6] Eschatology refers to the relationship of the present to the future of God's reign. The pastoral letter on the economy recognizes that the Christian lives in tension between the presence of the reign of God here and now begun and its fulfillment which will only come at the end of time. God's designs toward human life have been revealed throughout salvation history and uniquely in the life, death, and resurrection of Jesus; but the ultimate realization of the reign of God will come only at the end of time.

The question of eschatology, or the relationship between the reign of God and the present world, can be understood in terms of the five types relating Christ and culture proposed by H. Richard Niebuhr.[7] The Christ-against-culture model sees the reign of God in opposition to what exists at the present and serves as the basis for a radical opposition between the reign of God and existing institutions and realities. The Christ-of-culture model tends to identify the reign of God with present culture and grounds a Christian ethic of strong support for what exists at the present. Niebuhr then mentions three models in the middle ground between these two extremes. The eschatology proposed in the bishops' letter corresponds to Niebuhr's centrist model of Christ transforming culture. Such an appoach calls, in general, for transformation and change of the present but cautions against naively expecting any utopias to come into existence in this world. Within such an eschatological perspective the bishops are critical of the present structures, not radically opposed to them, and propose ways to change and modify existing policies and structures. The bishops recognize that their approach is reforming and pragmatic. A definite coherence is present between the eschatology briefly mentioned in the letter and the substantive positions taken on the American economy.

Three important ramifications of ecclesiology for social ethics and the teaching arc developed in the pastoral letter. The first aspect is intimately connected with eschatology and involves the understanding of Catholicism as a church and not a sect in the words of the typology developed by Max Weber. The sect type is distinguished by the fact that it is a relatively small group of believers striving to live the fullness of the gospel in a radical way in opposition to the world around them. The church type is more open to a wider membership, is less radical and rigorous in its ethic, and does not see itself in total opposition to the world around it. Whereas the sect type often accepts the Christ-against culture model, the church type cannot exist in such radical opposition to the existing culture.

The Roman Catholic Church not only belongs to the church type but might be the perfect illustration of such a type. The Catholic Church claims to have a universal mission and calls all to the church. It wants to embrace all peoples, all cultures, all languages, all continents. A church aspiring to such universality must recognize pluralism and diversity on a number of levels. The Catholic Church has insisted on doctrinal agreement but historically has been open to great diversity in the political, social, and economic orders. In fact, until the time of Pius XII it was generally accepted that Catholic thought was indifferent to political forms of government. The form of government was secondary to the requirements for justice within any and all forms of government.[8] The pastoral letter on the economy recognizes that the church is not bound to any particular economic, political, or social system or ideology. It has been constantly reiterated in church documents that room for diversity and pluralism exists in the church with regard to specific economic policies and institutions. However, some movements such as atheistic communism have been looked upon as inherently evil. Historically Roman Catholicism has embraced a wide range of opinions on social and economic questions and still continues to do so. The United States bishops in their two pastoral letters are very careful to point out the continuing place of pluralism and diversity in the church in judgments about complex, specific economic or political problems.

The understanding of mediation proposed earlier means that as one descends to the specific and the complex, one cannot claim to arrive at a certitude that excludes the possibility of error. The gospel-inspired approach mediated through reason and the empirical sciences and cognizant of all the relevant data involved cannot claim on specifics to be the only possible gospel-inspired answer. Thus, the pastoral letter distinguishes between the level of universal moral principles or formal church teaching and prudential judgments about specific policies. The latter do not carry the same moral authority as the former, and on this level of specific judgments and applications a rightful diversity of opinion can exist within the church. The bishops propose their judgments on these practical and specific issues and policies as being true and consistent with the gospel, but they recognize the possibility of disagreement on these judgments within the Christian community. This acceptance of mediation confirms the Catholic approach to ecclesiology that recognizes the diversity of positions on specific complex issues in the social and economic areas.

Perhaps the most significant ecclesiological aspect of the

two United States bishops' letters has been the manner in which these teaching documents have been prepared. A wide-ranging dialogue has been in process with all those who might have something to contribute to the documents — activists, academicians, businesspersons, labor leaders, economists, philosophers, theologians, scripture scholars, social scientists, politicians, government officials, and others. Symposia and conferences have been held at various Catholic and non-Catholic institutions of learning throughout the country. The drafts of the pastoral letter have been circulated publicly, and criticism has been welcomed from every conceivable approach. The very process itself has been a great teaching tool in terms of awakening consciousness both within the church and society in general to the moral issues involved in the United States economy. The dialogical and collegial teaching style of writing this document contrasts with the approach still used in most Catholic documents, especially those emanating from Rome. An increasing difficulty will be experienced in the future for church authorities to propose documents that have not been prepared with this same wide-ranging and public dialogue.

III. Different Levels of Ethical Discourse

Perhaps the most significant methodological aspect of the moral teaching proposed in the pastoral letter on the economy is the explicit recognition of the different levels of moral discourse in the letter itself. The acceptance of mediation and the need to distinguish the different levels of authoritative teaching in the document have obviously influenced a very explicit recognition of the various levels of moral discourse found in the letter itself. The systematic structure of the letter's ethical methodology goes from the more general to the more specific. This structure has basically stayed the same throughout the drafts, with one significant modification in the second draft.

In the last few decades within Roman Catholicism a shift in theology from classicism to historical consciousness has developed with a corresponding shift from a static and deductive methodology to a more inductive methodology. The Pastoral Constitution on the Church in the Modern World illustrates this newer approach by beginning the discussion of particular moral problems with an analysis of the signs of the times. The drafters of the pastoral letter feared that the move from the more general to the more specific as developed in the first draft gave the impression of being a totally deductive approach. At the same time this approach did not attract the average reader.[9] The solution in the second draft was to keep the approach of different levels moving from the more general to the more specific but to add a first chapter dealing with the signs of the times to point out the problems existing at the present and the need for a moral approach to these questions. The problem experienced by the drafters was certainly compounded by the fact that the one document tries to do so many different things. The letter wants to be sound from the viewpoint of systematic Catholic ethics, but at the same time it wants to capture the interest and enthusiasm of the general reader. These two goals are not always easily reconcilable in the same document.

In general I think it important that the letter does recognize the different levels of moral discourse, especially in light of the acceptance of mediation and the need to distinguish different levels of unity and diversity within the church. Such a reflective systematic approach does not have to be static and totally deductive, but this more scientific approach will not necessarily make exciting reading for everyone.

What are the different levels of ethical discourse distinguished and elaborated upon in the letter? As described in the terminology of the letter itself, the different levels are perspectives, the Christian vocation, ethical norms and principles, and, finally, specific judgments and policies on economic matters made in the light of the principles and other levels of ethical discourse. These four levels correspond to what I think are four very significant levels of ethical discourse — a basic perspective, the person as subject and agent, the principles and norms governing human existence, and concrete judgments. These four levels are similar to the four levels of moral discourse proposed by Unversity of Chicago Professor James Gustafson in his earlier work *Christ and the Moral Life.*[10] These four different levels of ethical discourse will now be discussed.[11]

Fundamental Perspective

The level of fundamental perspective is developed in the pastoral letter in terms of biblical perspectives with emphasis on the focal points of the faith of Israel and of the disciples of Jesus—creation, covenant, and saving history. This biblical perspective should inform the way in which Christians and the church approach all the issues involved in the economic order. Comparatively little has been discussed in contemporary Christian ethics itself about this fundamental level of ethical discourse which can go under such different names as perspective, posture, stance, or horizon. In the pastoral letter this level also seems to include the more general values, ideals, and goals which should influence economic policies and structures.

A comparatively slight but significant shift was employed after the first draft of the letter. The first draft developed a biblical vision or perspective for economic life, but for all practical purposes the use of the scripture in the first draft is only on this first level and is not incorporated into the other levels of ethical discourse. The second draft made some small attempts to employ the scriptures on the other levels of ethical discourse and did not completely limit the scriptural influence merely to a basic perspective. However, the basic perspective is developed exclusively on the basis of scripture.

The use of scripture in moral theology is a question that has recently received much attention, but no general agreement exists on exactly how the scriptures should be employed in moral theology. Catholic theology has rightly insisted that scripture is not the only source of ethical wisdom and knowledge for the Christian. In fact, as mentioned earlier, it was only after the Second Vatican Council that Catholic moral theology gave greater importance to the role and use of the scriptures in moral theology. In the light of the many sources of ethical wisdom and knowledge for the Christian and in the light of the hermeneutic problem of moving from biblical times to contemporary times, the role of the scriptures will be greater and more significant in the broader and more general levels of ethical discourse and less controlling and significant as one descends to the more specific. Thus, for example, one cannot prove the truth of a very concrete norm for the economy today because such was proposed as a concrete norm in very different circumstances in a particular biblical stituation. However, the general scriptural warning about the dangers connected with wealth and riches has a permanent validity for Christians in all ages.

On the level of basic perspective or stance we should expect a very great contribution from the scriptures, but I think that the basic perspective should be a systematically developed Christian perspective, one not based only on the bible. Such a Christian perspective is heavily dependent on biblical materials, but in the light of all the sources of moral theology it must go beyond only the biblical to involving the totality of the Christian perspective. In addition, some fundamental questions can be raised about the very enterprise of trying to construct a biblical theology. Such approaches are truly human constructs made by contemporary persons, and hence by their very nature they move beyond the biblical texts themselves.

The Person

The second level of ethical discourse is the level of the person with all the dispositions, virtues, and attitudes that should characterize the person, a level of discourse not explicitly mentioned in the first draft of the pastoral letter. In the second draft this level appears under the rubric "The Christian Vocation in the World Today" but still remains comparatively underdeveloped.[12]

No one can deny the importance and significance of this level of ethical discourse. The biblical metaphor teaches that the good tree brings forth good fruit, while the bad tree brings forth bad fruit. Good actions come from good persons. Philosophical reflection reminds us that the person is both subject and agent who by one's own actions contributes to what one is as a person and at the same time expresses one's personal reality in and through action.

The fact that this level of ethical discourse is so underdeveloped is consistent with the entire approach taken in the letter. For all practical purposes the letter deals with the changes that should be made in the existing economic structures and institutions so that they can better serve all human beings. These changes can primarily be brought about in and through the political order in all its different ramifications. Comparatively little is said about the day-to-day life of the people who are working in various capacities in the economic institutions and structures, and little is also said about these institutions themselves, such as the corporation or the business.

One of the most significant constraints facing the drafters of the pastoral letter was the fear of making the document too long. Excessive length was a basic complaint that was made after the first draft of the letter. As a result the drafters could not include too many things in their letter. The small section dealing explicitly with the level of the person did appear in the second draft. However, that this whole aspect could not be brought out in greater detail remains unfortunate. Not only is this an important level of ethical discourse and of moral living, but emphasis on this level shows the important role played by the laity and all the people of God in the economic realm. The day-to-day life of people in the economic order does not receive as much attention as it should.

Yet my remarks should not be misinterpreted. Some critics in the United States have maintained that the responsibility for involvement in economic life and in economic policies and issues belongs first of all to the laity. The bishops should teach principles but should not get into the specifics of economic policies and judgments.[13] I strongly disagree with this understanding. From my perspective more importance in a letter of this type must be given to the day-to-day Christian existence of those who spend their life working one way or another in the economic sector. Yes, the letter contains appeals to workers, owners, and managers, but needed is more attention to the work that is daily done in the economic sector and to the vocation of all Christians working there. Especially a document addressing itself to the members of the church and not just attempting to make a contribution to the public policy debate should give more attention to what most of the people in the church community do in their daily lives. As it stands, the public policy aim of the letter controls its content and development to the detriment of the role of the believing members of the church community in their everyday work.

Principles and Norms

The third level of ethical discourse concerns the principles and norms that should direct economic policy and structures. The bishops strongly emphasize this level as distinguished from the level of prudential judgments and applications made in the light of these principles and norms. The letter itself highlights a number of these principles such as justice and human rights, but other important principles from the Catholic tradition are also involved in the letter. This section will now briefly consider what seem to be the most important principles in the Catholic tradition's teaching on economic policies and structures — the role of the state, justice, human rights, preferential option for the poor, and the universal destiny of the goods of creation to serve the needs of all.

ROLE OF THE STATE. The Catholic tradition understands the state as a natural society, based on the social nature of humankind, uniting persons in a political society to achieve the common good. The common good is not opposed to but includes the good of the individual person. The state consequently is seen, not as something bad or evil which restrains and coerces, but as something basically good which contributes to the benefit and fulfillment of all its individual members. This understanding of the state based on the social nature of humankind avoids the two opposite dangers of laissez-faire individualism and collectivism. The state recognizes and protects the basic rights of individual persons and of the lesser associations and groups that comprise the total fabric of society. The principle of subsidiarity governs the proper role and function of the state, which exists especially to help persons and lesser associations and groups, but in contemporary times official Catholic teaching has recognized that the growing socialization in human relationships calls for a greater role for the state.

JUSTICE. Corresponding to the three different types of relationships existing within society are three different types of justice. Commutative justice governs the relationship of individuals to individuals and is described as impartial and blind to personal differences, being characterized by an emphasis on arithmetic equality. For example, if I borrow five dollars from you and five dollars from the richest person in the world, I owe each of you the same amount — five dollars. Distributive justice governs the relationship of society to individuals in properly distributing goods and services. Distributive justice is not blind but must take account of persons, so that it involves proportional and not arithmetic equality. In distributing various burdens society must take into account the abilities of individuals to contribute. Thus, progressively higher taxes should be paid by those who earn more, and jobs involving the public trust should be given only to those capable of carrying out their responsibilities effectively. In distributing goods a number of canons should govern proper distribution, but human needs constitute a basic criterion. Every human being has a right to that basic level of human goods which is necessary for a minimally decent human existence. What is just from the viewpoint of distributive justice is not the same for all but is proportionate to the needs and abilities of the persons involved. Note again the social aspect of distributive justice and that distributive justice calls not for equal distribution for all but only for a basic minimum for all.

Social justice governs the relationship of individuals to society and again is characterized by a proportional equality and by the need to take account of persons and their differences. In discussing social justice the bishops emphasize participation, which has been an aspect developed only recently in the Catholic social tradition. To participate in the total life

of society is a right based on social justice, with a corresponding duty of society and all others to recognize and facilitate
this right of participation. Social justice governs the contribution that each makes to the good of the whole.

HUMAN RIGHTS. Official Catholic teaching only embraced
and elaborated on the concept of human rights in the encyclical
Pacem in terris of Pope John XXIII in 1963.[14] The Catholic
tradition had previously emphasized duties and shied away
from rights language as being too closely identified with the
thought of individualistic liberalism. However, in defense
against the abuses of totalitarianism Catholic social thought
came gradually to champion human rights. Human rights are
ultimately based on the dignity of the human person. Along
with its perennial recognition of the social aspect of human
nature recent Catholic teaching in emphasizing human rights
has insisted not only on political and civil rights which have
traditionally been espoused by Western liberalism but also
economic and social rights. Economic rights converge with
the traditional emphasis on distributive justice to underscore
the fact that every human person has a right to those material
goods that are necessary to live a minimally decent human
existence.

OTHER PRINCIPLES. Recent Catholic theology with its shift
to a more direct relationship of the gospel and faith to daily
life has accented the preferential option for the poor. The
privileged place of the poor in the reign of God is accentuated
throughout the Hebrew and Christian scriptures. Liberation
theology in South America has developed this concept at great
length, which has also become a part of recent official Catholic
social teaching. This preferential option is not exclusive and
thereby confirms the more philosophical emphasis on distributive justice and human rights. Recent Catholic social teaching
has also insisted on the traditional teaching that the goods of
creation exist to serve the needs of all. All other rights, including those of private property and of free commerce, are
to be subordinated to this primary finality of the goods of
creation.

All these principles tend to put more emphasis on the social aspects of human existence than is generally found in the understanding prevalent in the American ethos. This social emphasis is the basis for many of the concrete judgments made in the letter itself and for the need to regulate the activity of individuals and markets in order to achieve the common good of all.

The fourth level of ethical discourse is that of concrete judgments about economic structures and policies in the light of the principles and other levels of ethical discourse. The letter considers four specific areas of concern—employment, poverty, food and agriculture, and the relationship of the United States to the world economy. Included also is a more future-oriented chapter dealing with economic policy under the rubic of a call for a new American experiment involving partnership for the public good. An investigation of the particular judgments and policies proposed in these areas lies beyond the scope of this particular study.

IV. An Unresolved Tension

Catholic social teaching and social ethics have generally deemphasized the role of power and conflict in bringing about social justice and social change. The tradition has constantly emphasized the harmonious working together of all for the common good. Society was often described in terms of organic metaphors with all the parts working together for the good of the whole. Catholic ethics insisted on the importance of reason and the goodness of human reason and downplayed the role of sin, which could very well serve as a grounding for greater conflict in society. Only very recently has this body of teaching begun to recognize the importance of participation by all. Catholic ecclesiology even today does not want to make differences on specific economic policy and structures into reasons for division within the church. As a result, then, these differences are seen as examples of pluralism rather than emphasizing the basic conflicts created by them.

In my judgment a greater place for power and conflict in

bringing about social change must be recognized than the Catholic tradition has been willing to admit. Conflict must always be only a strategy and can never become an ultimate. Likewise conflict and power must always be in service of the common good and not of selfish interests. However, experience and reality point to a greater role for conflict and power in bringing about social justice and change than the Catholic tradition in general and the bishops' letter in particular are willing to admit explicitly.

However, the letter contains some emphases that open the door to recognizing a greater role for conflict. The letter stresses the importance of the participation of all in the life of society. The bishops freely talk about the need to overcome the powerlessness and the marginalization of many people in our society. Also frequent references to power itself exist. All these indications point to the fact that the letter should explicitly acknowledge a greater role for power and conflict in bringing about social change than now appears explicitly in the letter itself.

V. Conclusion

This chapter has explained and analyzed the Christian social ethical methodology as found in the pastoral letter on the economy and in the Catholic tradition in general. Presuppositions, theological contexts, the different levels of ethical discourse, and an unresolved tension have been examined in an attempt to analyze and explain how religious ethical inquiry is related to economic policy in this letter in particular and in contemporary Catholic social ethics in general.

NOTES

1. John F. Cronin, *Social Principles and Economic Life*, rev. ed. (Milwaukee: Bruce, 1964), pp. 30, 31.

2. *Gaudium et spes*, par. 43, in David J. O'Brien and Thomas A. Shannon, eds., *Renewing the Earth: Catholic Documents on Peace,*

Justice, and Liberation (Garden City, NY: Doubleday Image, 1977), p. 217.

3. Pope John XXIII, *Pacem in terris*, especially par. 1-7; O'Brien and Shannon, *Renewing the Earth*, pp. 124-126.

4. 1971 Synod of Bishops, *Justitia in mundo*, in O'Brien and Shannon, *Renewing the Earth*, p. 391.

5. For a discussion of many aspects of this question see Charles E. Curran and Richard A. McCormick, eds., *Readings in Moral Theology No. 2: The Distinctiveness of Christian Ethics* (New York: Paulist Press, 1980).

6. National Conference of Catholic Bishops, *Pastoral Letter on Catholic Social Teaching and the U.S. Economy: Second Draft* (Washington, DC: National Conference of Catholic Bishops, 1985), par. 61-62, pp. 123-124.

7. H. Richard Niebuhr, *Christ and Culture* (New York: Harper Torchbooks, 1956).

8. Cronin, *Social Principles and Economic Life*, p. 281.

9. Rembert G. Weakland, "The Economic Pastoral: Draft Two," *America* (September 21, 1985): 129-130.

10. James M. Gustafson, *Christ and the Moral Life* (New York: Harper and Row, 1968), p. 240.

11. Explicit references will be to the second draft of the letter, which is all that is available at the present time. This differentiation of the four levels has been so central to the first two drafts that one can rightly assume that the final document will follow the same approach.

12. NCCB, *Pastoral Letter on Catholic Social Teaching, Second Draft*, par. 63-68, p. 20.

13. For approaches tending in this direction see J. Brian Benestad, *The Pursuit of a Just Social Order: Policy Statements of the U.S. Catholic Bishops, 1966-1980* (Washington, DC: Ethics and Public Policy Center, 1982); Russell Barta, ed., *Challenge to the Laity* (Huntington, IN: Our Sunday Visitor, 1980).

14. Pope John XXIII, *Pacem in terris*, par. 11-27, in O'Brien and Shannon, *Renewing the Earth*, pp. 127-130.

9: The Difference between Personal Morality and Public Policy

Catholic theology has traditionally recognized the very important distinction between the realm of morality and the realm of legality or public policy. What is true in the personal moral order is not by that very fact necessarily to be incorporated into law. However, at times the legal order and the moral order are the same.

The most controversial issue facing United States Catholicism in the legal order has been the issue of abortion. In the last three presidential elections the controversy over abortion laws has surfaced. Many Catholics, together with many others, have worked for a constitutional amendment to overturn the 1973 Supreme Court decision and to change present liberal abortion laws in the United States. However, some Catholics, including many respected Catholic politicians, have supported the existing abortion laws and funding by pointing to a distinction between the legal order and the moral order. The hierarchical leadership in the Catholic Church in the United States has consistently spoken out against the existing laws and has worked to change them.

The controversial question of abortion legislation and public funding came to the surface again in 1983 in the case of Sister Agnes Mary Mansour. Agnes Mary Mansour, a Sister of Mercy, was appointed director of the Department of Social Services of the State of Michigan in late 1982. Her local bishop, Archbishop Szoka of Detroit, claimed that she could not have his approval for this position unless she publicly opposed Medicaid funding for abortion. Without this permission she would, according to the bishop, be acting contrary to the church law and discipline. Agnes Mary Mansour maintained that she was morally opposed to abortion but could tolerate Medicaid funding for abortions for poor women through the Department of Social Services which she headed. The basic areas of disagreement are clear in this case, although some of the particulars are disputed.[1]

On May 9, 1983, Bishop Anthony Bevilacqua, serving as the Ad Hoc Delegate of the Vatican, delivered to her a mandate from the Holy See. The mandate from Rome demanded that in virtue of her vow of obedience she immediately resign her position as director of the Department of Social Services of Michigan. Faced with this mandate, Sister Agnes Mary Mansour asked for a dispensation from her vows and is thus no longer a Sister of Mercy.

This unfortunate and tragic case has raised a number of very significant issues. This short chapter will concentrate on only one of these issues — the understanding of the relationship between the legal order and the moral order.

Public statements in the case of Sr. Agnes Mary Mansour unfortunately have not always recognized this traditional distinction. The archbishop of Detroit claimed that Sr. Mansour's refusal to state her opposition to Medicaid abortion payments for the poor was "contrary to the magisterium." Bishop Anthony Bevilacqua began his explanation of the Mansour case by stating: "There are two major issues. The basic and doctrinal issue is that of abortion. While Sr. Agnes Mary Mansour stated that she was against abortion, she refused to make a public statement opposing public funding for abortions and, in fact, supported such funding. . . .The second major issue is a disciplinary one, that of disobedience."[2]

All Catholics recognize the teaching function of the hierarchical magisterium in matters of faith and morals. In Catholic self-understanding, doctrine refers to a belief officially taught by the church. But the question of abortion legislation or the public funding of abortion does not come under these categories. Public policy in this matter involves many prudential judgments about which there can be no doctrine or magisterial teaching on faith and morals.

Respected Catholic theologians and philosophers such as John Courtney Murray and Jacques Maritain have tried to explain in a systematic way what is the basis for the difference between the personal moral order and the legal order. Murray develops his approach in the light of the position of many Protestant ethicists who are disturbed by the gap between public policy, or the way the state behaves, and personal morality. Murray firmly rejects the dichotomy between "moral man" and "immoral society" made famous by Reinhold Niebuhr. Niebuhr's Christian realism justifies society's need to do some things (e.g., violence, spying) which are in a sense morally wrong. Morality in the Catholic tradition is determined by the ends and the relevant orders of political and individual reality. The end and order of political and social reality are different from the end and order of individual and personal reality.[3]

Murray would certainly recognize an overlap between the two, but in his book he stresses the differences between public policy and private morality. "It follows, then, that the morality proper to the life and action of society and the state is not univocally the morality of personal life, or even of familial life. Therefore the effort to bring the organized action of politics and the practical art of statecraft directly under the control of the Christian values that govern personal and familial life is inherently fallacious. It makes wreckage not only of public policy but also of morality itself."[4]

Jacques Maritain spells out the same basic difference between political and individual ethics. The French philosopher seeks a middle ground between political hypermoralism and political amoralism. Politics is a branch of ethics, but as a branch it is specifically different from the other branches on the same stem. "For human life has two ultimate ends, the one subordinate to the other; an ultimate end *in a given order,* which is the terrestrial common good, or the *bonum vitae civilis;* and an *absolute* ultimate end, which is the transcendent, eternal common good. An individual ethics takes into account the subordinate ultimate end, but *directly* aims at the absolute ultimate one; whereas political ethics takes into account the absolute ultimate end, but its *direct aim* is the subordinate ultimate end, the good of the rational nature in its temporal achievement. Hence a specific difference of perspective between those two branches of ethics."[5]

Thus Maritain morally justifies in political ethics the use of intelligence methods and coercive police measures; selfishness and self-assertion which would be blamed in individuals; a permanent distrust and suspicion; a cleverness not necessarily mischievous but yet not candid with regard to the other states; the toleration of certain evil deeds by the law; the recognition of the principle of the lesser evil and the *fait accompli* (the so-called "statute of limitations").[6]

These two spokespersons of the Catholic theological and philosophical traditions thus indicate the differences between individual and political morality and trace the difference to the different ends and different orders involved. However, the Catholic tradition has not only recognized the differences between the two orders but has also tried to indicate more precisely what is the relationship between them.

Thomas Aquinas in his *Summa theologiae* attempts to show the relationship between the moral and the legal orders. Thomas poses the question primarily in terms of the relationship between natural law and positive law, or human civil law. Human civil law is ordered to the common good (note the emphasis on ends and ordering), but not all the acts of all the virtues are capable of being ordered to the common good.[7] Thomas also recognizes the need for a realistic approach to civil law. Laws are to be applied according to the human condition. Civil laws should suppress only the more grievous vices from which the majority of human beings can abstain.[8]

Thomas mentions another important aspect of civil law when discussing the question of whether the religious rites of infidels should be tolerated in society. Thomas responds that human government is derived from divine government and should imitate it. Even though God is omnipotent, God still permits certain evils to occur in the world which the divine power could prohibit. God permits such evil lest greater goods would be taken away or greater evils would follow. Thus the ruler and governors of human society can tolerate certain evils lest greater good would be impeded or greater evils would occur. Here Thomas cites Augustine's famous justification of the toleration of public prostitution.[9] Thus Thomas indicates the importance of different prudential judgments in determining what is civil law.

The Second Vatican Council touches on the question of the relationship between law and morality in its discussion of religious liberty. Here the Thomistic approach of toleration is somewhat transformed in the light of a more systematic understanding of the role and function of law in a limited constitutional form of government. The Declaration on Religious Freedom accepts as its fundamental criterion for law that the freedom of human beings is to be respected as far as possible and curtailed only when and insofar as necessary. The end of the state is public order, and this order thus becomes the criterion justifying the need for law. Public order consists of an order of justice, which safeguards the rights of all individuals in society, an order of peace, which enables human beings to live harmoniously in society, and an order of public morality understood as the minimum of public morality necessary for people to live together in society. Note that the end of public order is more limited than the end of the common good. The common good is the end of society itself, but public order is the end of the limited constitutional state which is only a part of society.[10] The acceptance of the concept of public order does not deny the older common-good tradition but modifies it by explicitly recognizing that a limited constitutional government has an end which is more limited than the end of temporal society itself.

In addition to the two criteria of as much freedom as possible and of public order to guide the coercive intervention of the state through law, in my judgment two other aspects must also enter into the complete determination of what is good law. First of all the law as such must be equitable and enforceable. If a law cannot be equitably enforced, it is not good law. In addition, law-making involves a pragmatic aspect. Sometimes one will not be able to enact a law that one considers ideal but will have to settle for some type of compromise. At other times one might have to conclude that working for a particular law or piece of legislation is not feasible because no realistic chance exists for passing such a law.

The four criteria proposed here for the determination of civil law are by necessity somewhat broad and include a number of practical and prudential judgments about which people of good will can disagree.

In the matter of abortion law and public funding differing judgments result in different positions. One could readily maintain that a constitutional amendment is required to protect the rights of the fetus, since a primary aspect of public order is to protect human rights, especially the rights of those who are defenseless. Others might argue that in the light of the difference of opinion within American society on the exact status of the fetus, one should give the benefit of the doubt to the freedom of women in this area or recognize that attempts to change the present abortion law will not be feasible or successful. On the public-funding question it is quite easy to see how those opposed to abortion could be opposed to public funding of abortion. However, others could argue that poor people should not be discriminated against either in respect to more affluent people or in respect to medical procedures which they might want for themselves.

The purpose of this chapter is, not to take sides on the issue of the public policy and public funding of abortion, but to explain the relationship between morality and law. Personal morality cannot be made directly into law. The four criteria and the practical and prudential judgments involved in determining what constitutes good law mean that even within the Catholic Church different possible approaches will be adopted. Yes, bishops and church leaders can take a position on these issues, but they must realize that they are not teaching here in the same way they teach on faith and morals. They are dealing with the much more complex case of law and public policy. Catholics can and will continue to disagree about abortion laws and the public funding of abortion.

Recent statements by American Catholic bishops are in accord with the analysis just given. Recently the American Catholic bishops supported the proposed Hatch amendment to the Constitution which would give Congress or the several states the power to limit and prohibit abortions provided that a state law which is more restrictive than a law of Congress shall prevail. Many "Right-to-Life" advocates and even some bishops objected to supporting such an amendment precisely because it would allow some abortions. They wanted an amendment that would not allow any direct abortions.[11] Apparently the United States bishops made the prudential judgment that a stronger amendment was not feasible and had no chance of becoming law at the present time. Others concluded that even the Hatch amendment has no realistic chance of being passed as an amendment to the Constitution.

The last chapter pointed out that in their recent pastoral letters on peace and the economy the United States bishops recognize that the application of principles involves different possible prudential judgments and interpretations by people of good will. The specific public policy judgments made in these letters, for example, no first use of nuclear weapons, fall into such a category, so that other Catholics might disagree with the position taken by the bishops. These recent statements by the United States bishops are in line with the traditional understanding of the complex relationship between law and morality and with the more systematic analysis of good law developed here.

The second part of this book has attempted to explain the understanding of social morality in the Roman Catholic tradition as this tradition has continued to develop. One of the most significant developments in this tradition has been the increased importance given to the role of freedom in human society. The seventh chapter pointed out that the Catholic emphasis on human rights only came to the fore in the 1960s with this changed recognition of the importance of human freedom. Today human freedom in society has a much greater role than was recognized in earlier Catholic teaching. The changed teaching on religious liberty at the Second Vatican Council illustrates this development. The greater role of freedom in human society in general and in the state in particular reinforces the important distinction and difference between personal morality and social morality. However, freedom is not an absolute, and it must always be seen in the light of the common good of human society in general and of the public order of the state as such.

The contemporary challenge for Catholic social and political ethics is to give a greater importance to freedom without denying its traditional emphasis on the social nature of human persons and the fact that individual human persons ultimately need the social and political orders for their own good. Social or political morality can never be totally identified with personal or individual morality, but human persons need to construct a social order that recognizes both freedom and justice.

The one modification I would make in the understanding of law proposed in the Declaration on Religious Freedom is to give more explicit importance to the role of law in achieving social justice understood in a broad sense. The declaration itself sees the first component of public order as safeguarding the rights of all citizens. Some might be tempted to employ this concept of justice and rights to limit the role of the state in its work for social justice. The earlier chapters have insisted that on the basis of the principle of subsidiarity the government at times must directly intervene when individuals and lesser groups are unable to achieve the requirements of social justice. A proper understanding of public order is totally consistent with the interpretations of the principle of subsidiarity developed in the preceding chapters. The second part of this book has thus tried to show the principles which should govern life in society and in the state and also to apply these principles to some pertinent problems facing United States society today.

NOTES

1. See *Origins* 13 (September 1, 1983): 197-206, for the history and chronology of events in this case as presented by Bishop Bevilacqua, Agnes Mary Mansour, and the Detroit Provincial Team of the Sisters of Mercy of the Union.

2. Ibid., p. 197.

3. John Courtney Murray, *We Hold These Truths: Catholic Reflections on the American Proposition* (New York: Sheed and Ward, 1960), pp. 275-294.

4. Ibid., p. 286.

5. Jacques Maritain, *Man and the State* (Chicago: University of Chicago Press, 1951), p. 62.

6. Ibid., pp. 62, 63.

7. Thomas Aquinas, *Summa Theologiae* (Rome: Marietti, 1952), I-II, q. 96, a. 3.

8. Ibid., I-II, q. 97, a. 2.

9. Ibid., II-II, q. 10, a. 11.

10. Declaration on Religious Freedom, par. 7, in Walter M. Abbott, ed., *The Documents of Vatican II* (New York: Guild Press, 1966), pp. 685-687.

11. James Castelli, "Hatch Amendment Still Splits Pro-Life Camp," *Our Sunday Visitor* 70 (January 17, 1982):6.

Index